21.30

GUY DELISLE

ALBERT
AND THE OTHERS

GUY DELISLE

ALBERT
AND THE OTHERS

PETITS LIVRES

OTHER D+Q BOOKS BY GUY DELISLE:
PYONGYANG: A JOURNEY TO NORTH KOREA
SHENZHEN: A TRAVELOGUE FROM CHINA
ALINE AND THE OTHERS

DRAWN & QUARTERLY / PETITS LIVRES
P.O. BOX 48056
MONTREAL, QUEBEC
CANADA H2V 4S8
www.drawnandquarterly.com

ORIGINALLY PUBLISHED IN FRANCE BY L'Association.
FIRST DRAWN & QUARTERLY / PETITS LIVRES EDITION: NOVEMBER 2007.
ISBN 978-1-897299-27-2

DRAWN & QUARTERLY ACKNOWLEDGES THE FINANCIAL SUPPORT OF THE
GOVERNMENT OF CANADA THROUGH THE BOOK PUBLISHING
INDUSTRY DEVELOPMENT PROGRAM (BPIDP) AND THE CANADA
COUNCIL FOR THE ARTS FOR OUR PUBLISHING ACTIVITIES.

PRINTED BY IMPRIMERIE GAUVIN IN GATINEAU, QUEBEC, NOVEMBER 2007.

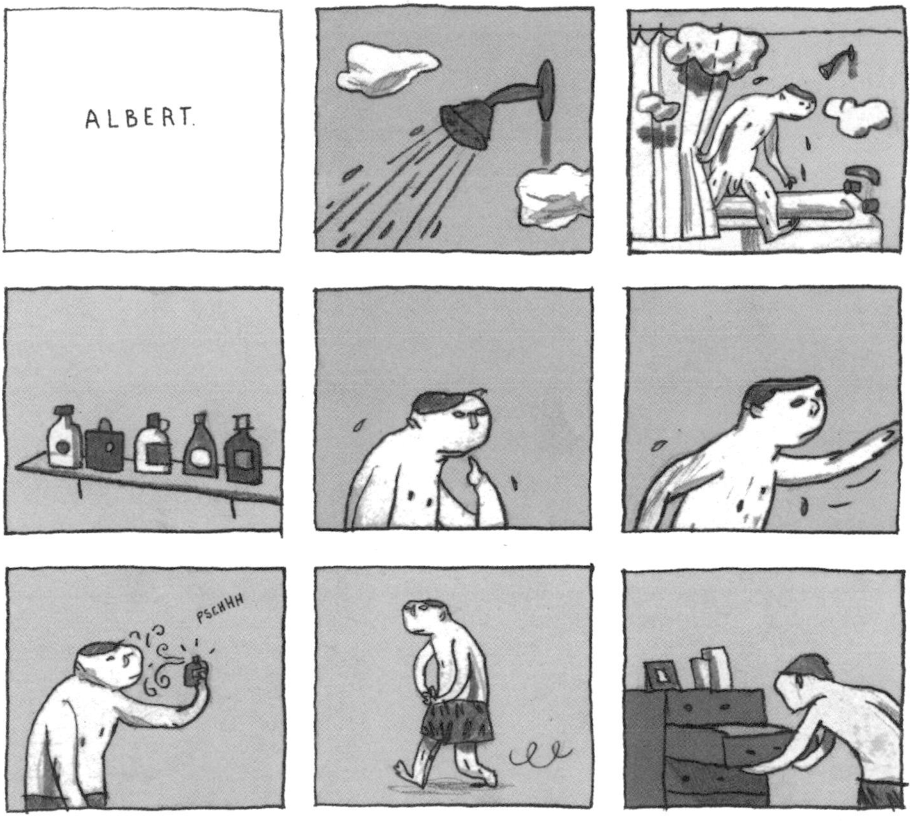
ALBERT.
PSCHHH

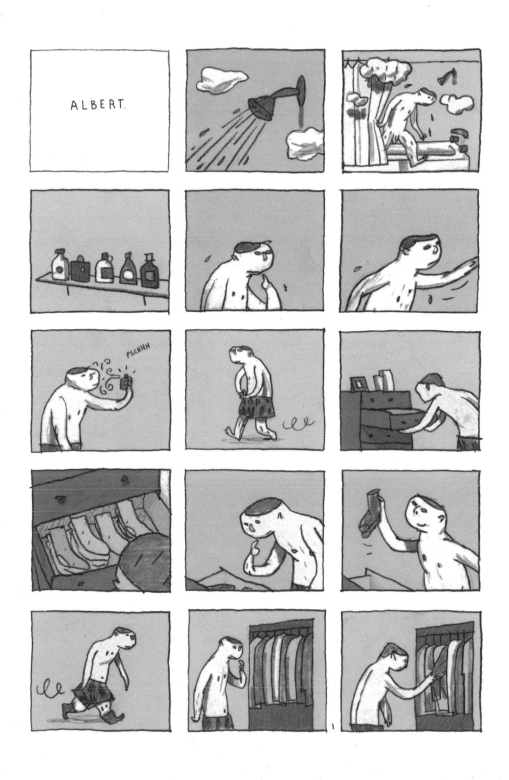

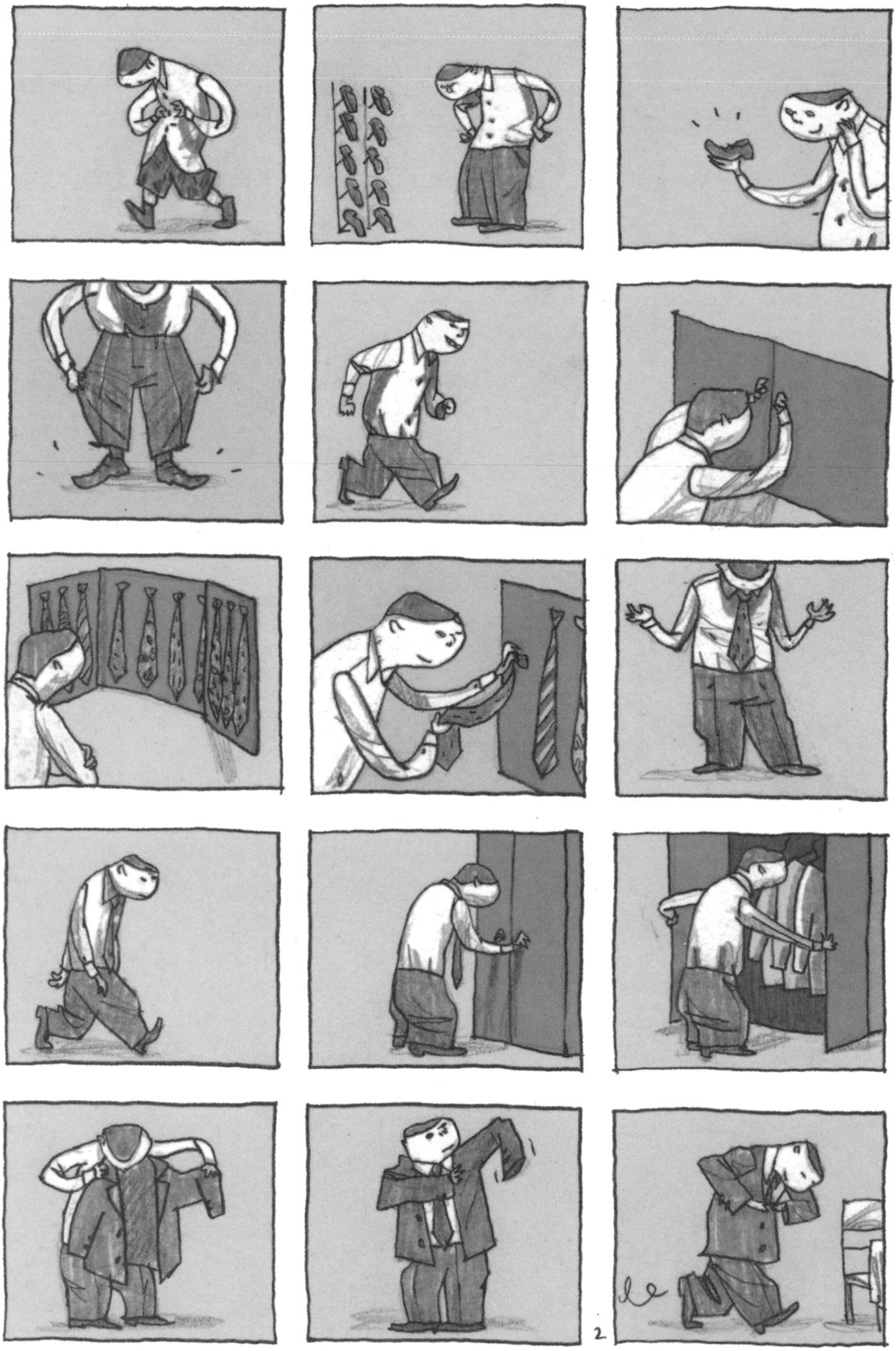

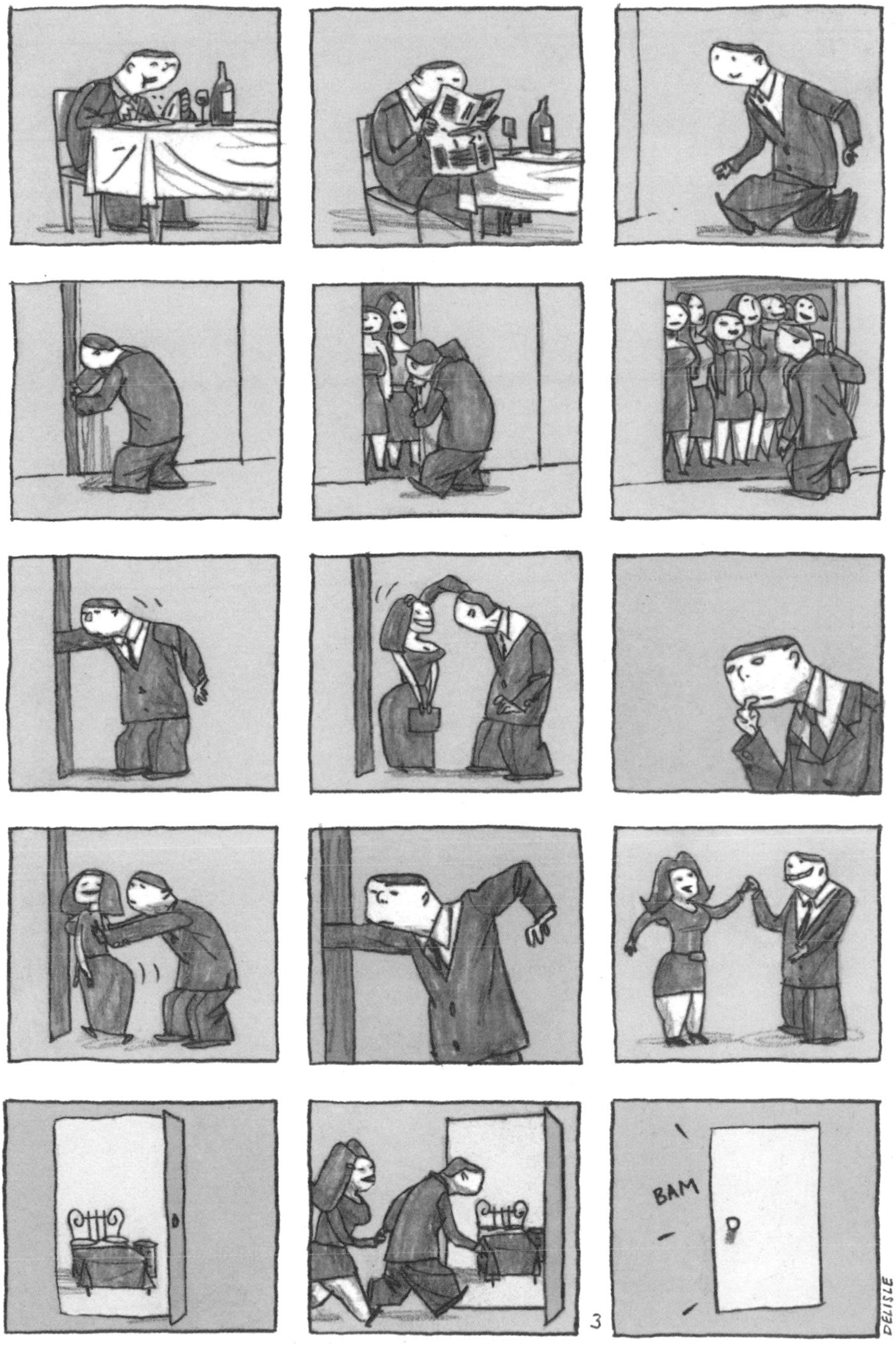
BAM
DELISLE

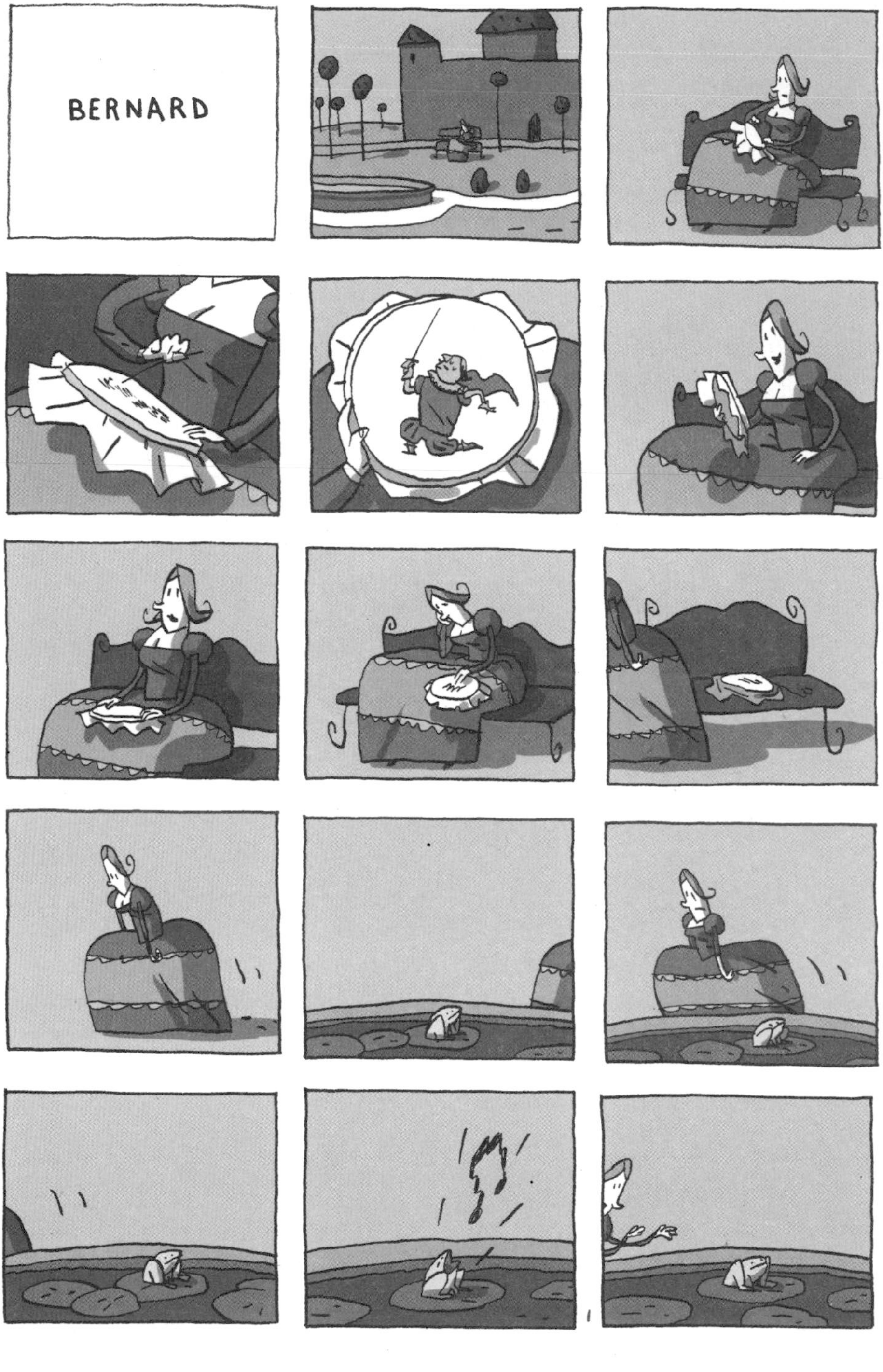
BERNARD

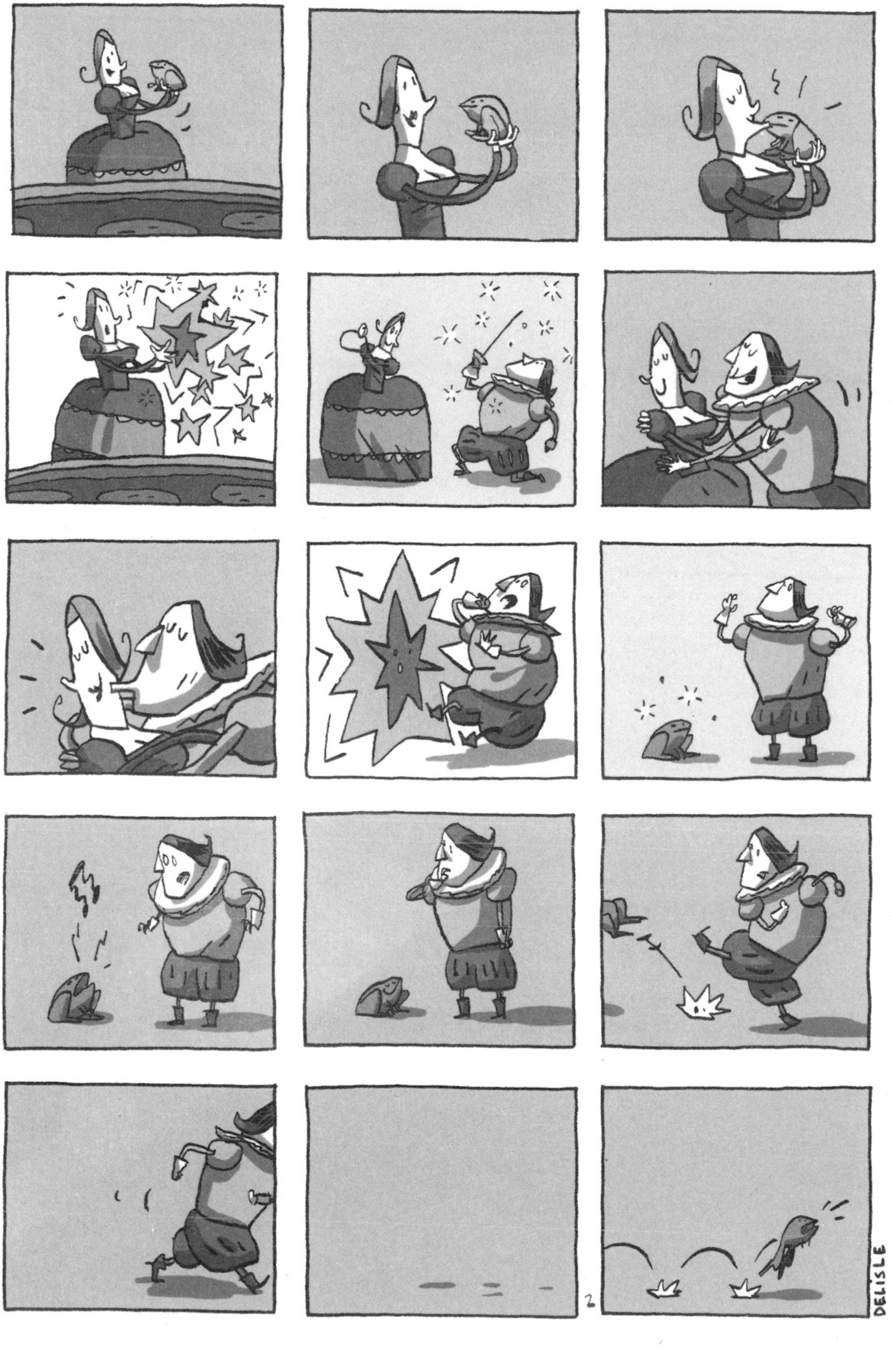
DELISLE

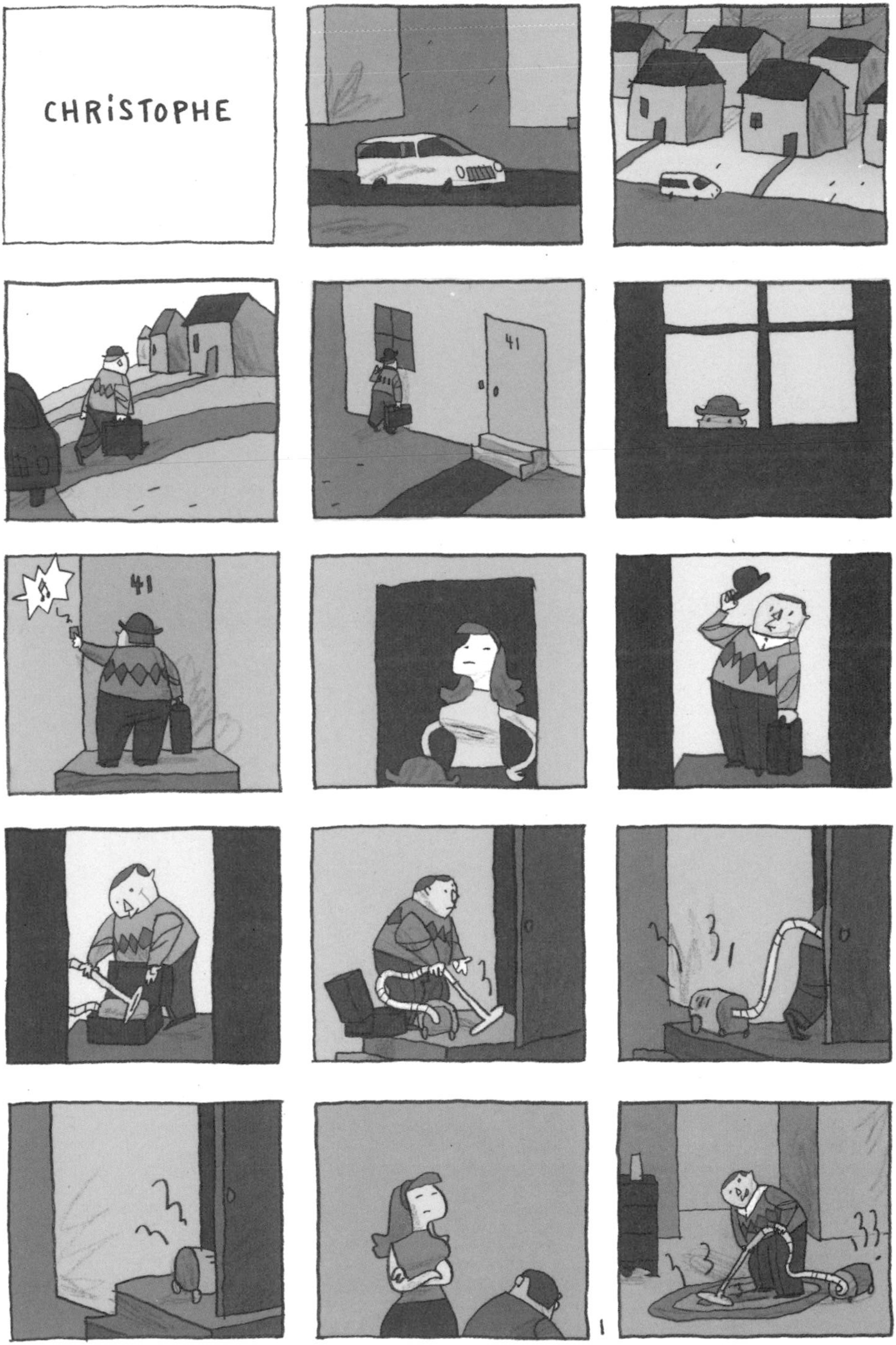
CHRISTOPHE
41
41

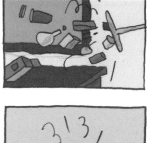

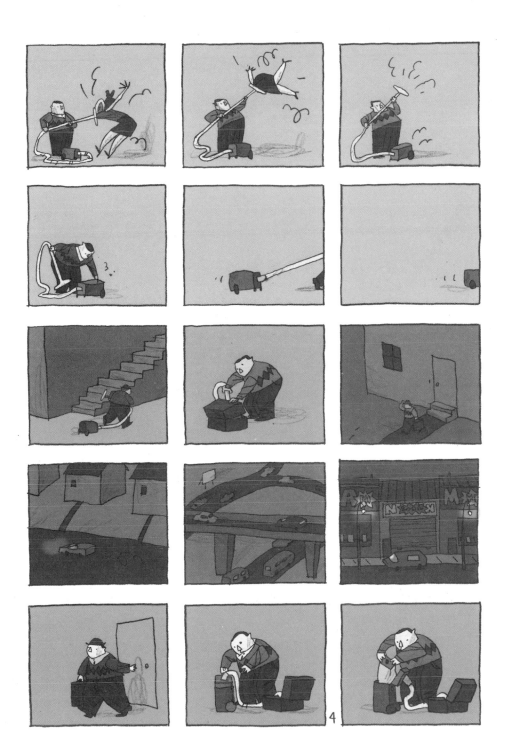

4

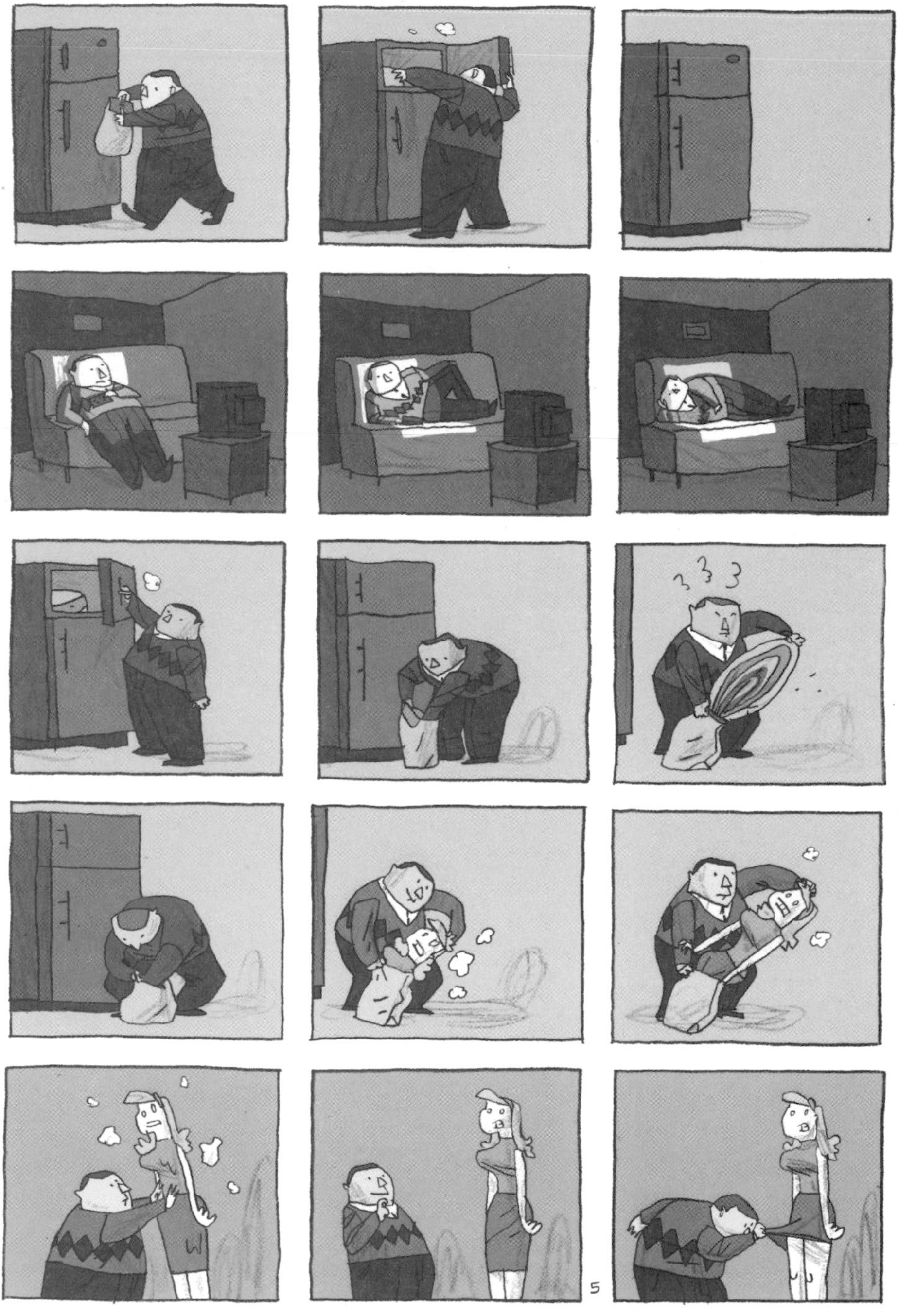

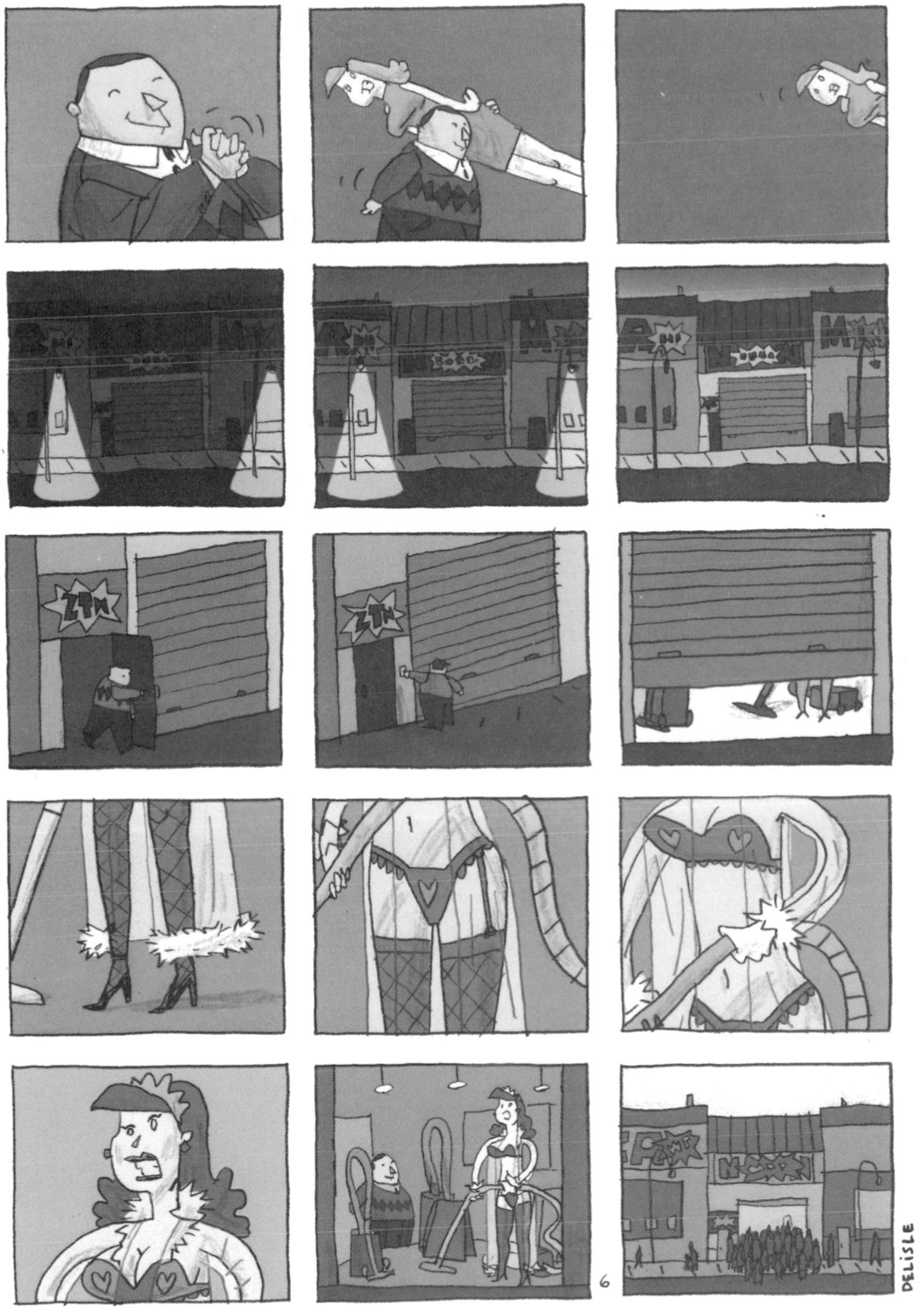
ZTM
DELISLE

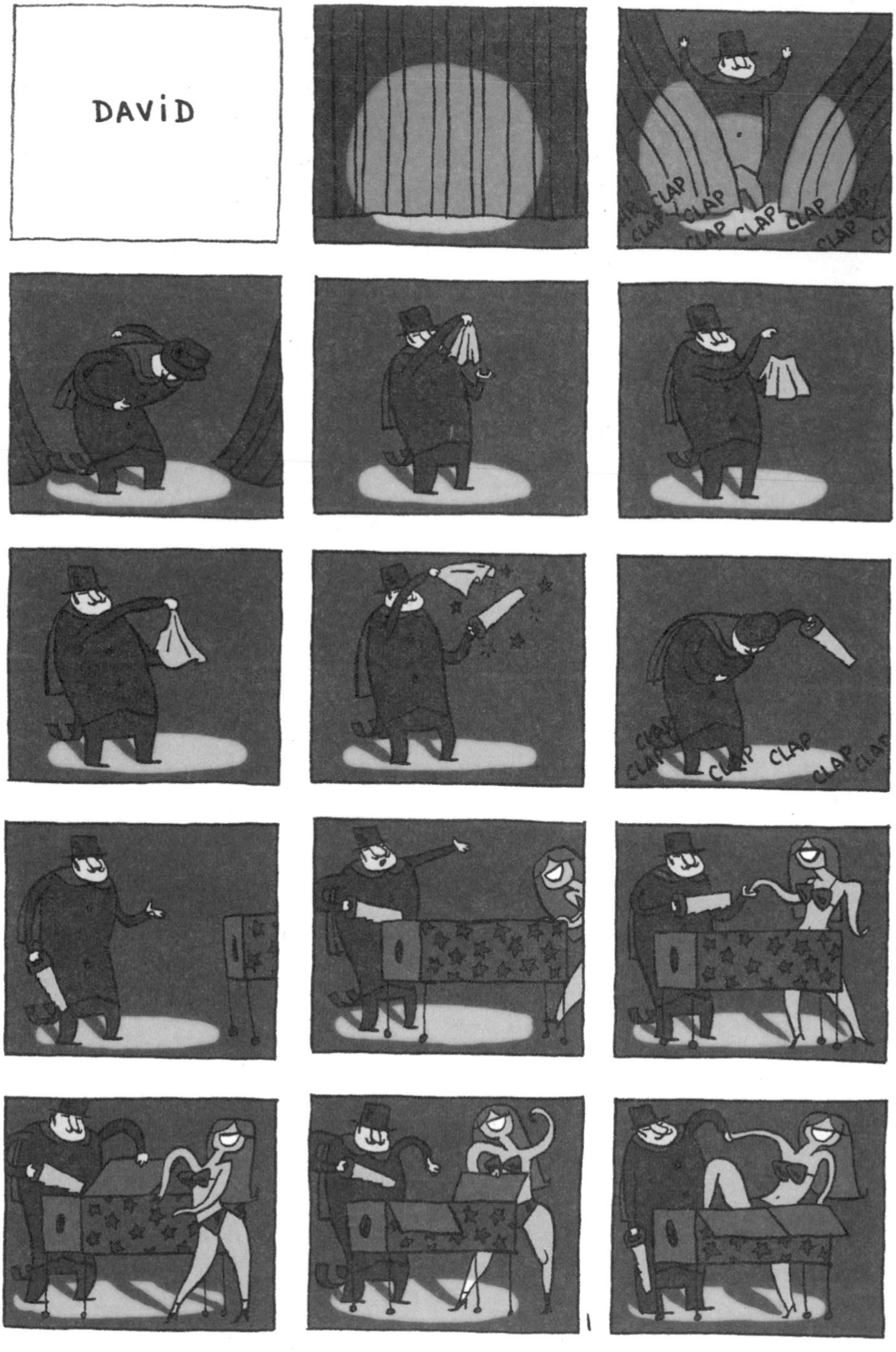
DAVID
CLAP CLAP CLAP CLAP CLAP CLAP CLAP CLAP
CLAP CLAP CLAP CLAP CLAP

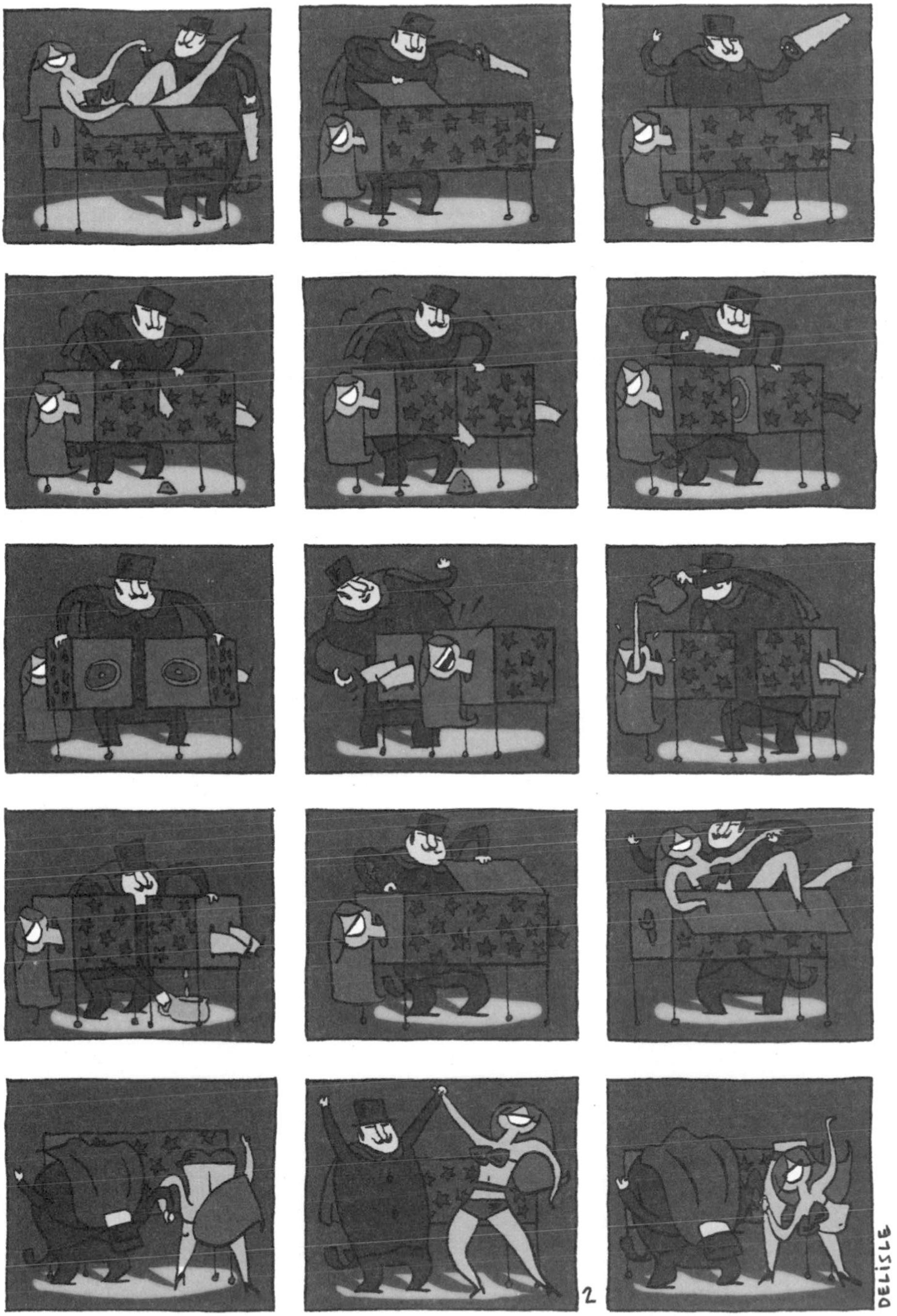
DELISLE

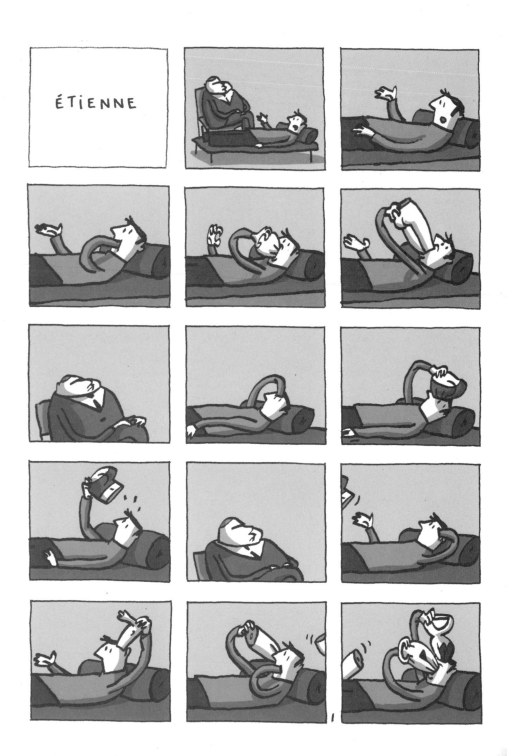

ÉTIENNE

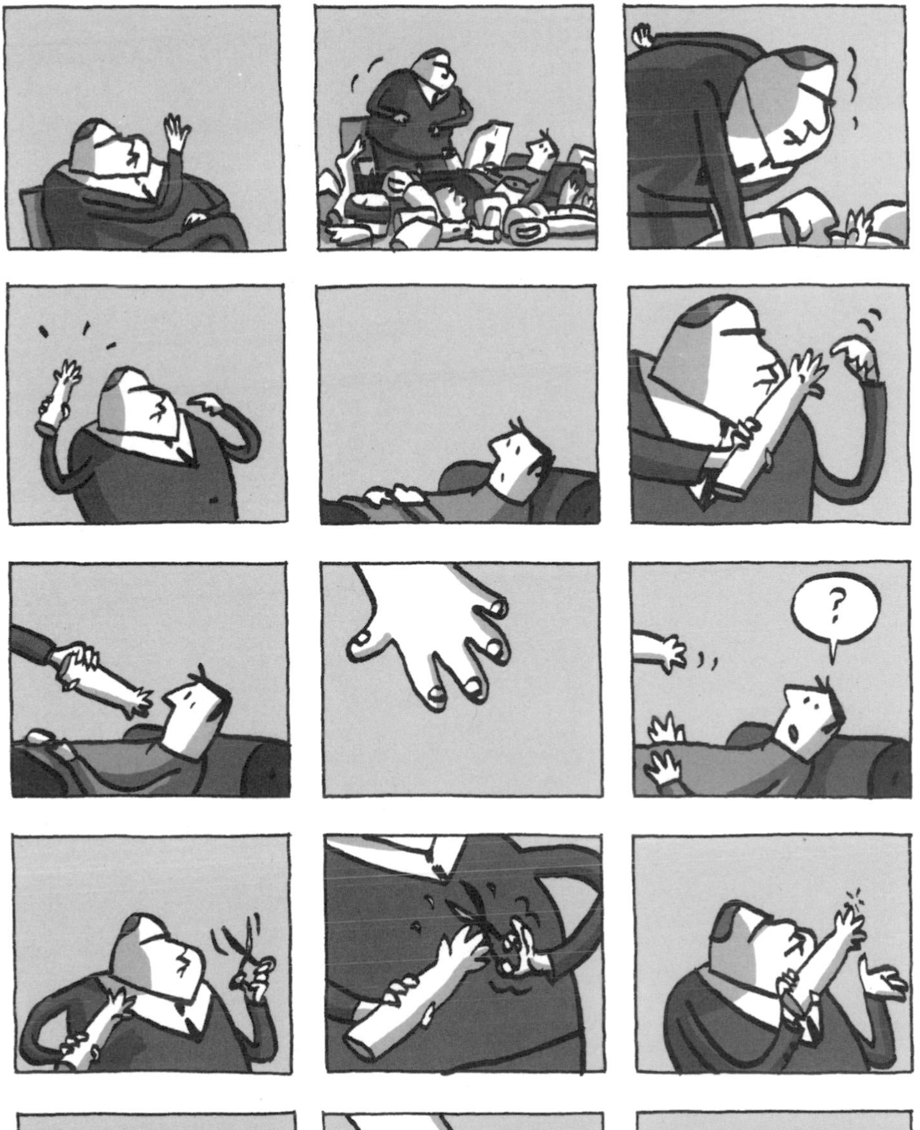
?

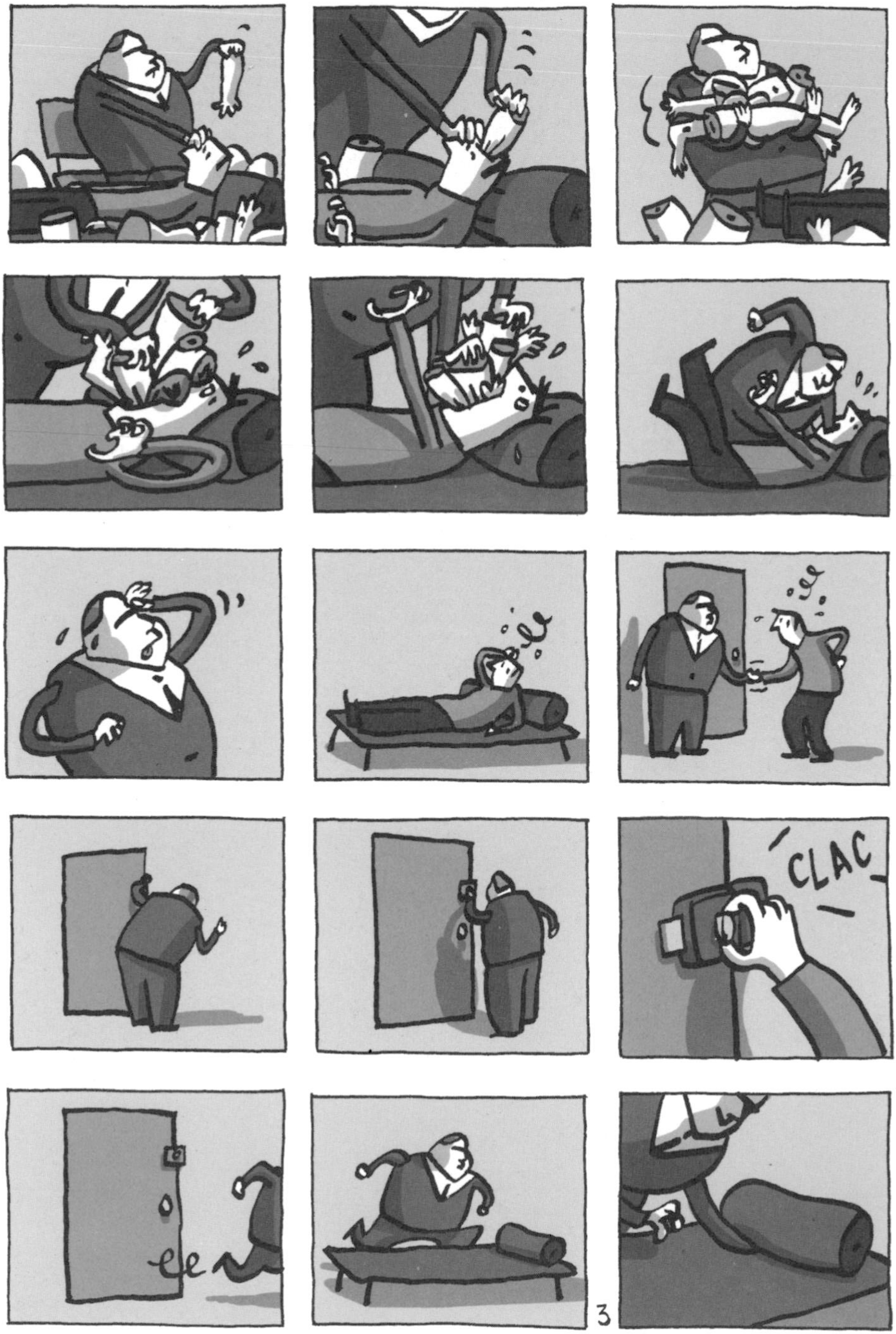
CLAC

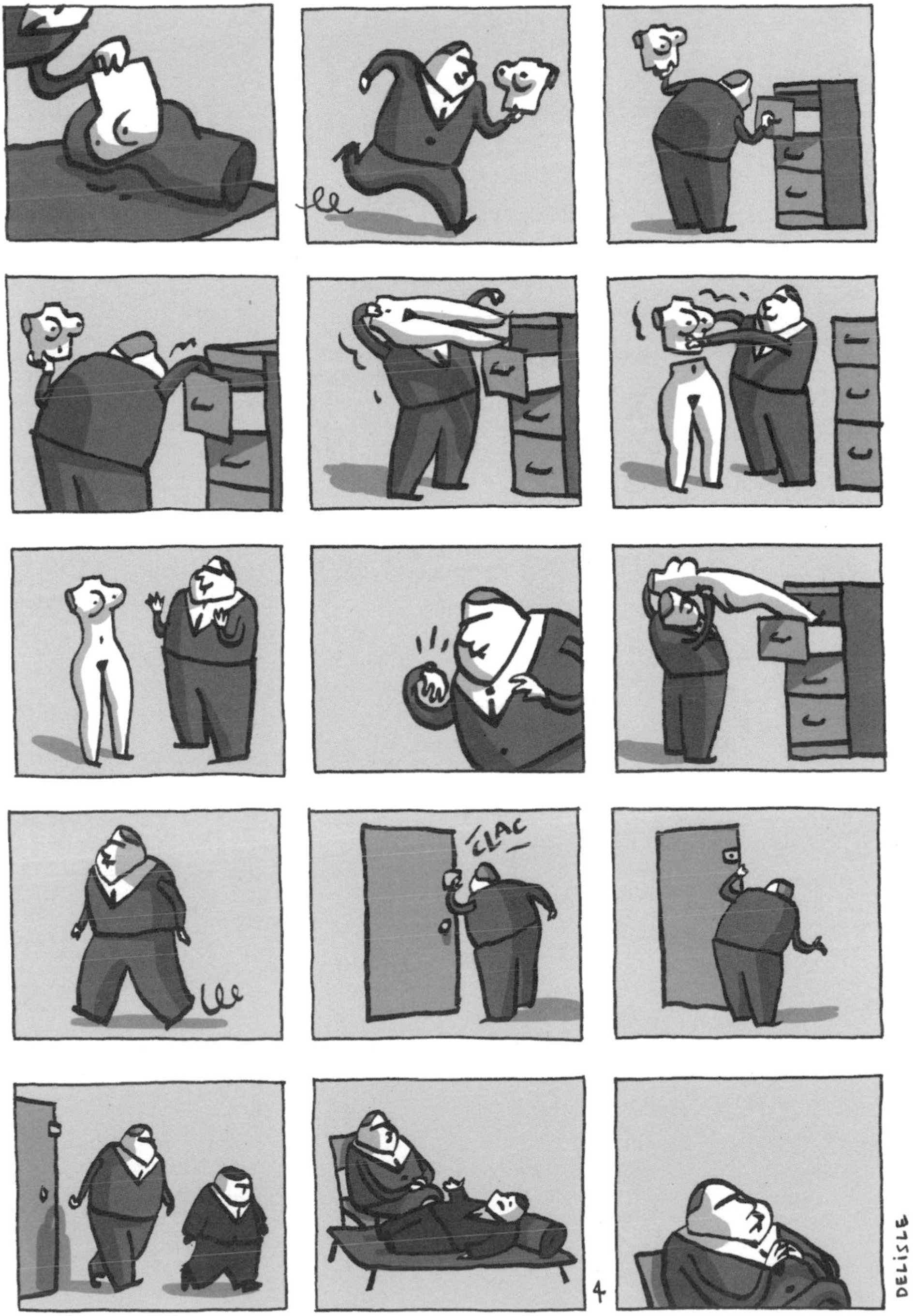
CLAC
4
DELISLE

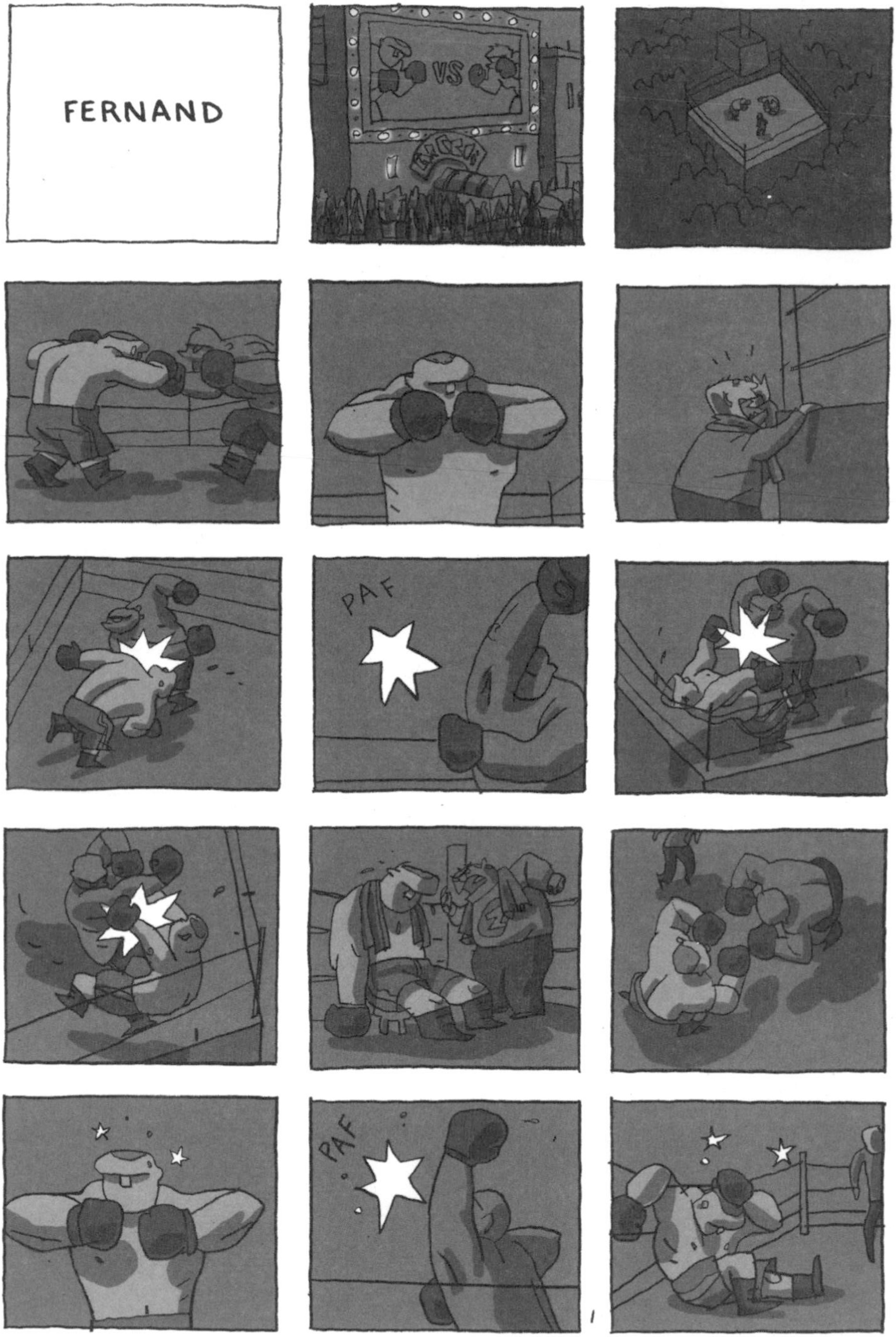
FERNAND
PAF
PAF

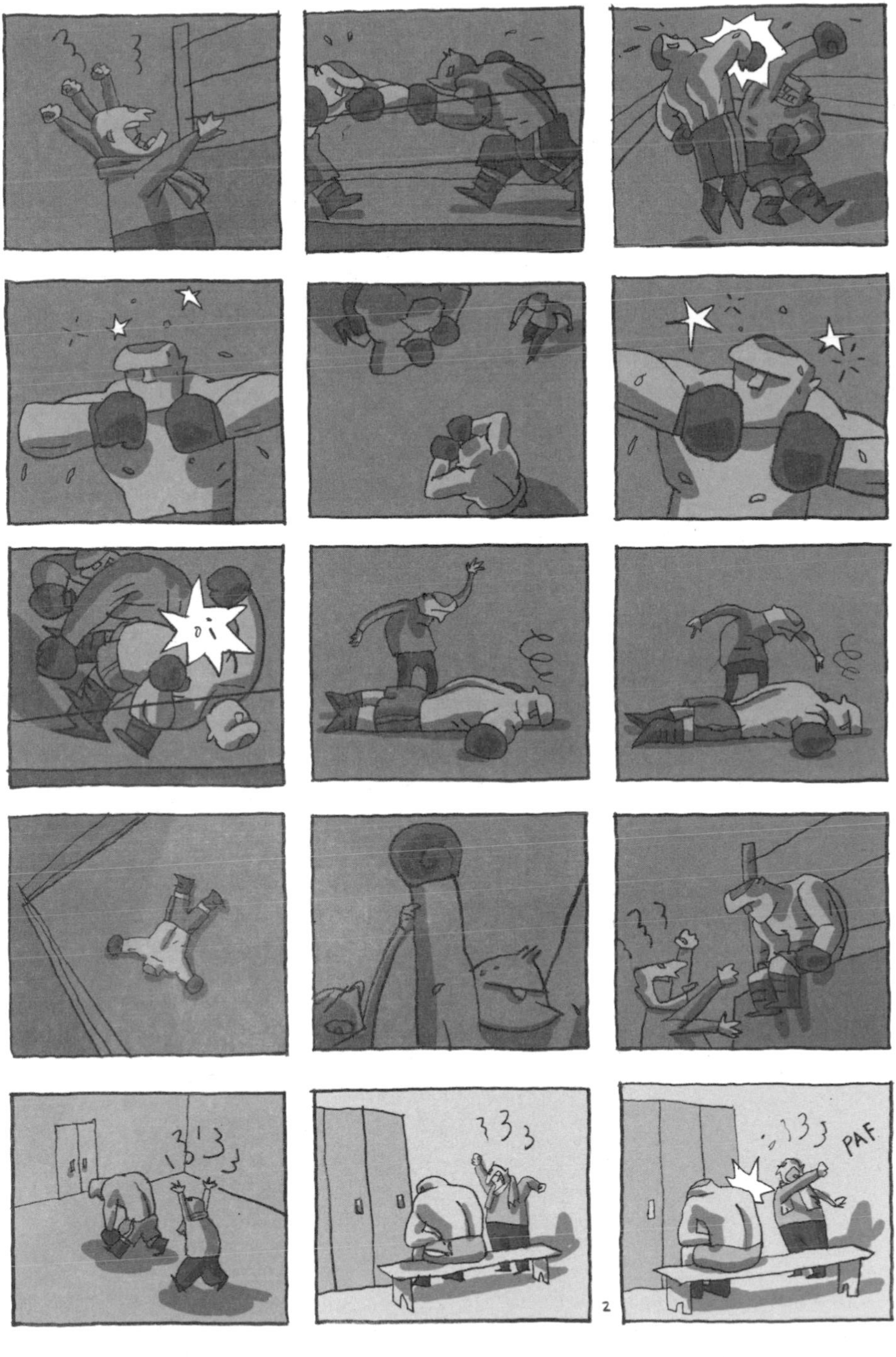
PAF

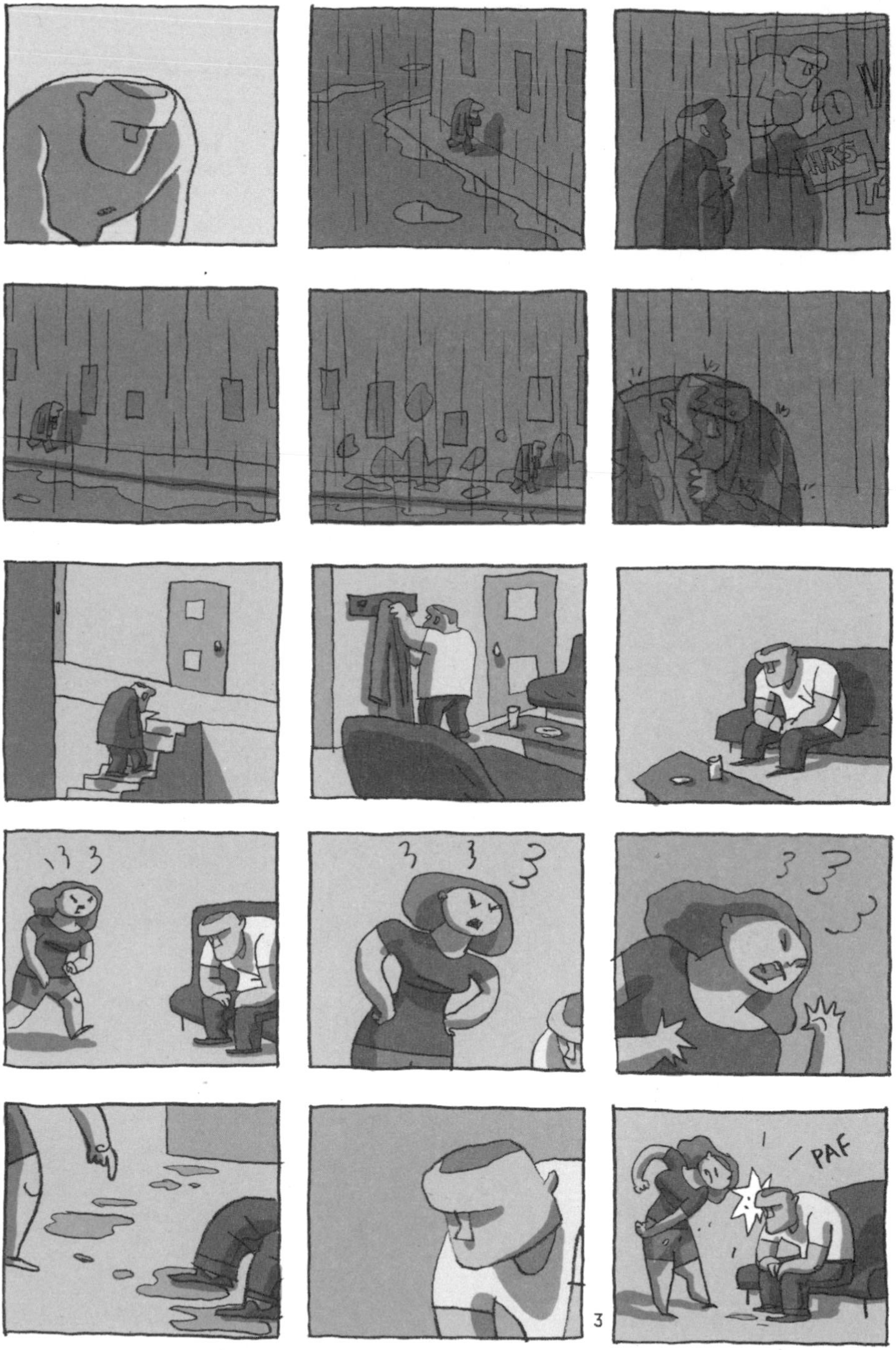
HRS
PAF

CLAC

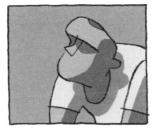

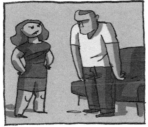

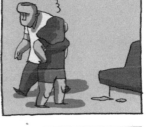

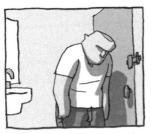

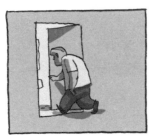

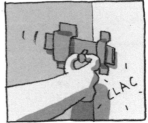

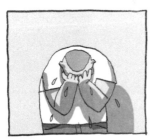

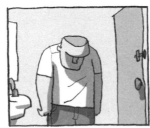

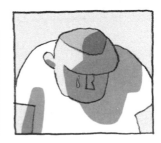

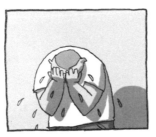

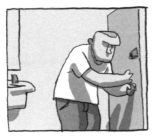

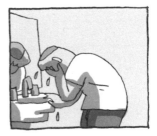

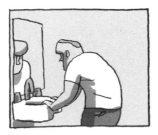

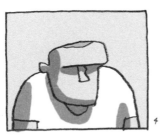

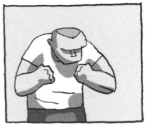

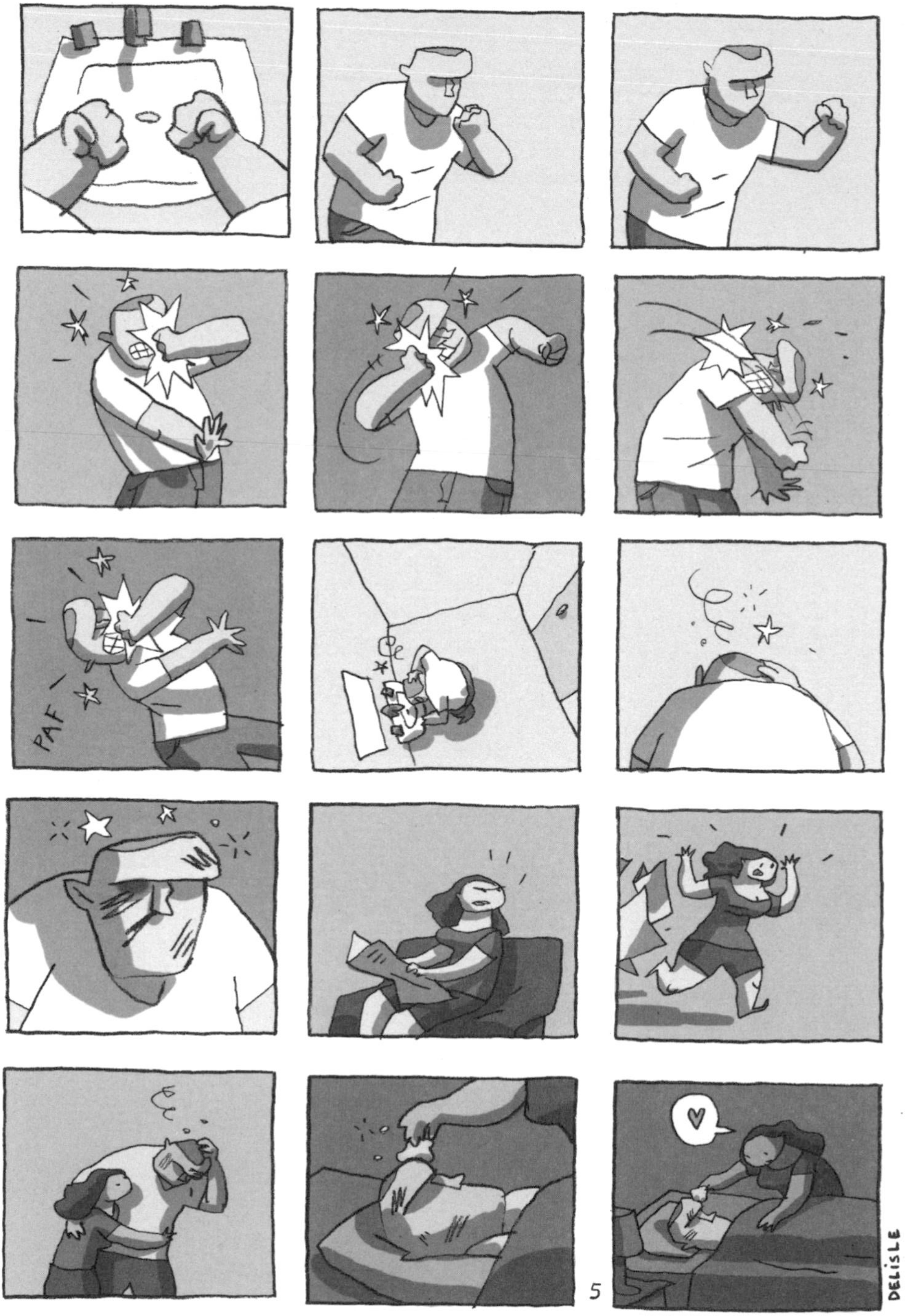
PAF
DELISLE

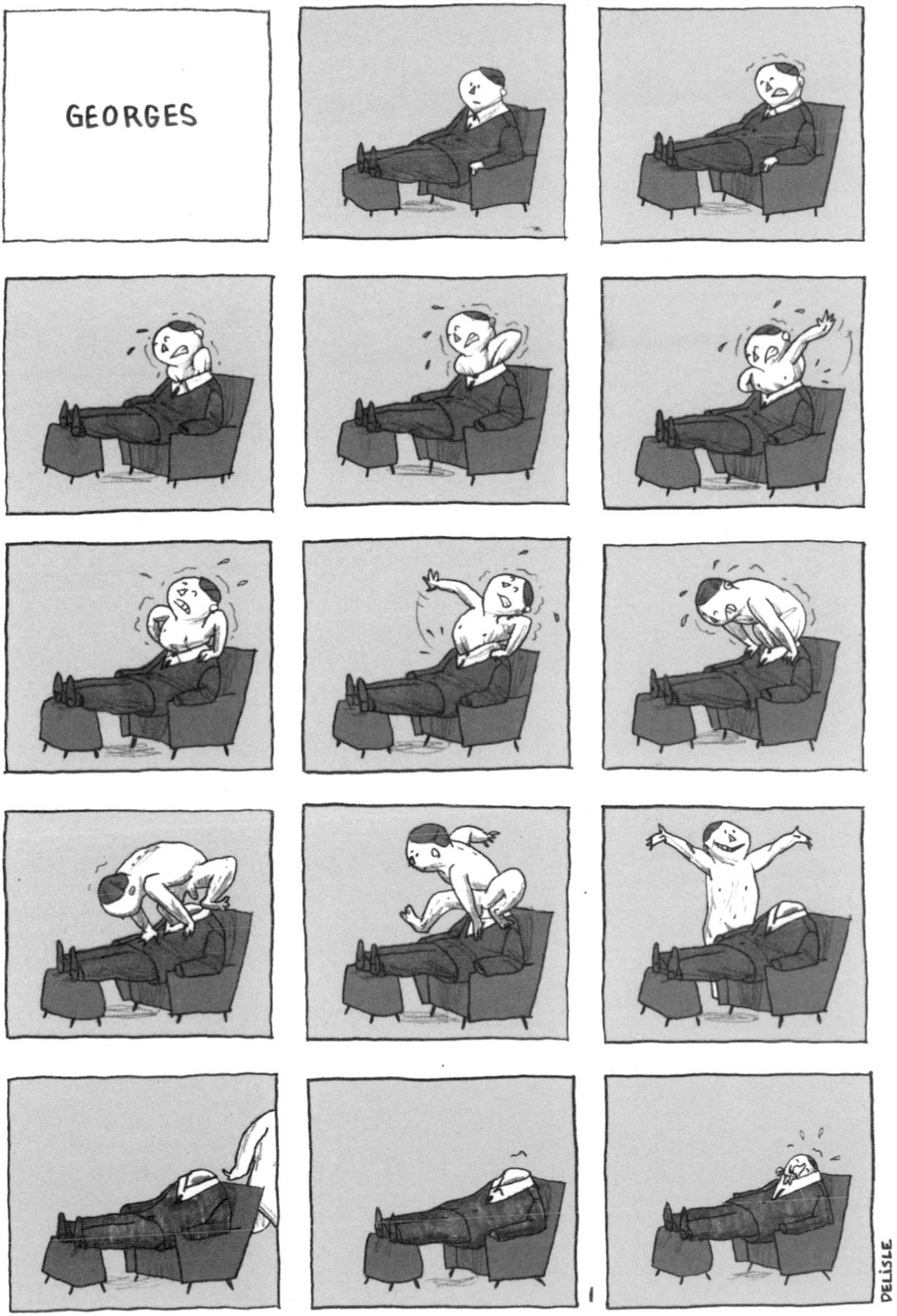
GEORGES
DELISLE

HENRI

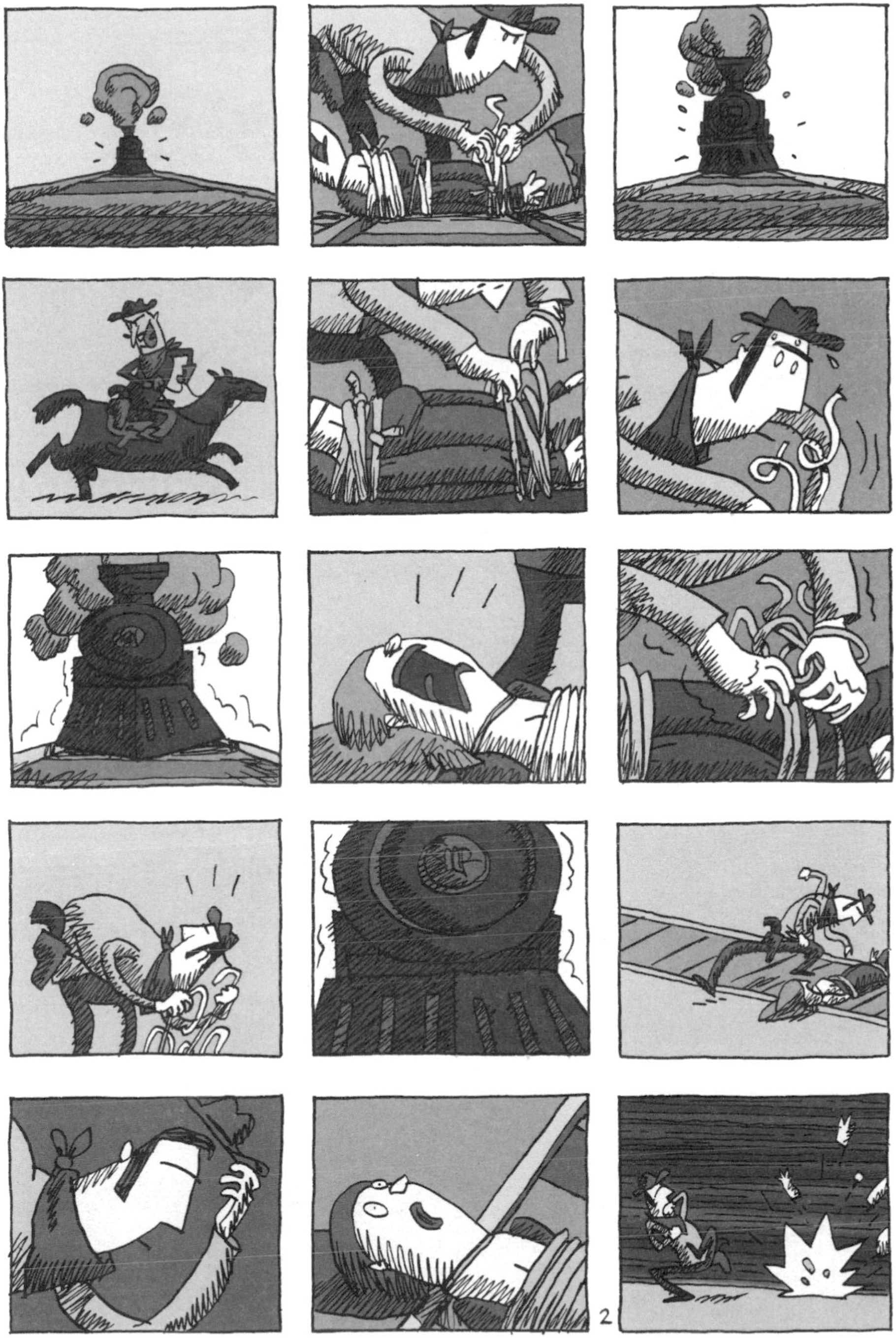

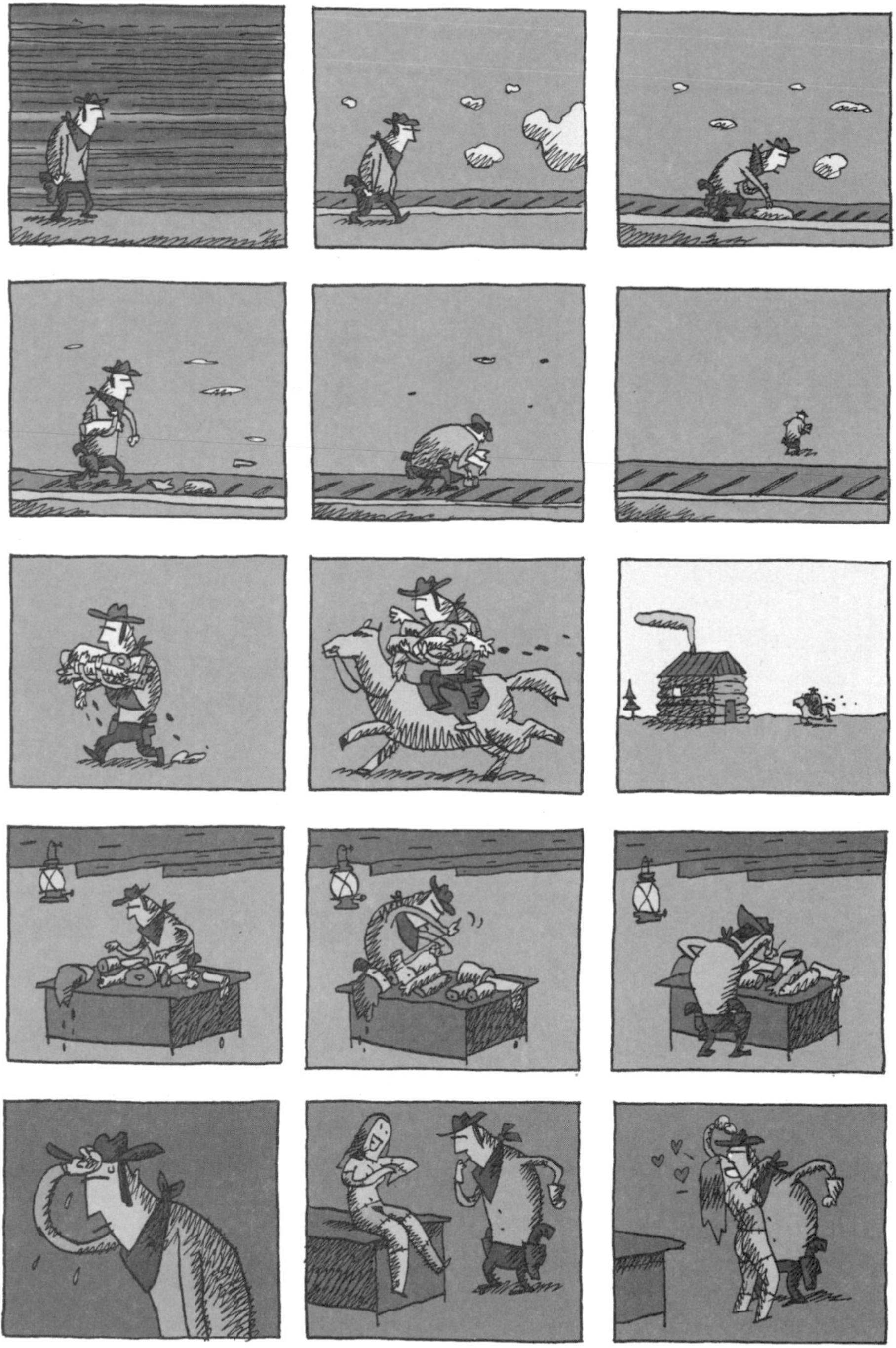

4

DELISLE

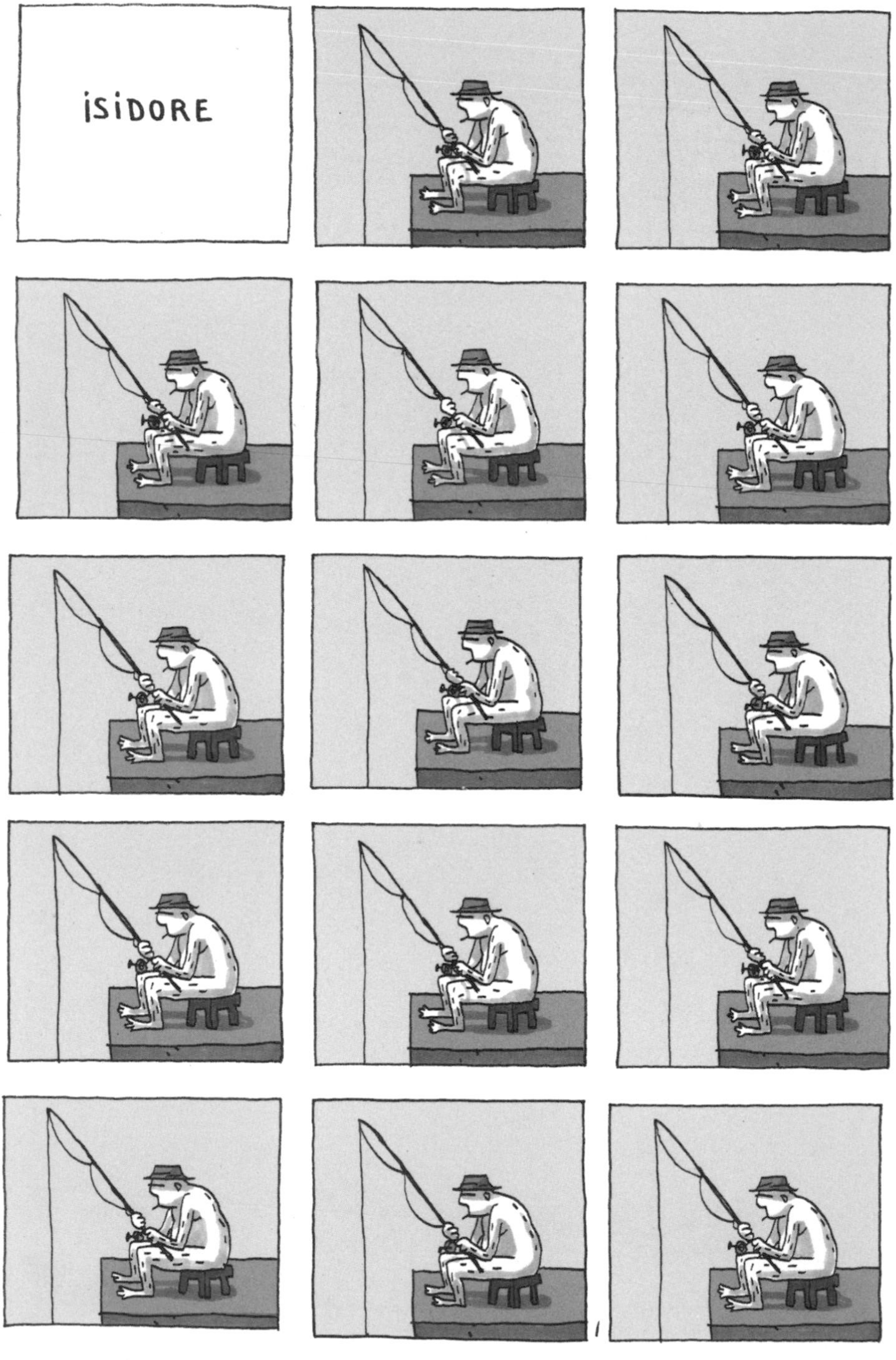
ISIDORE

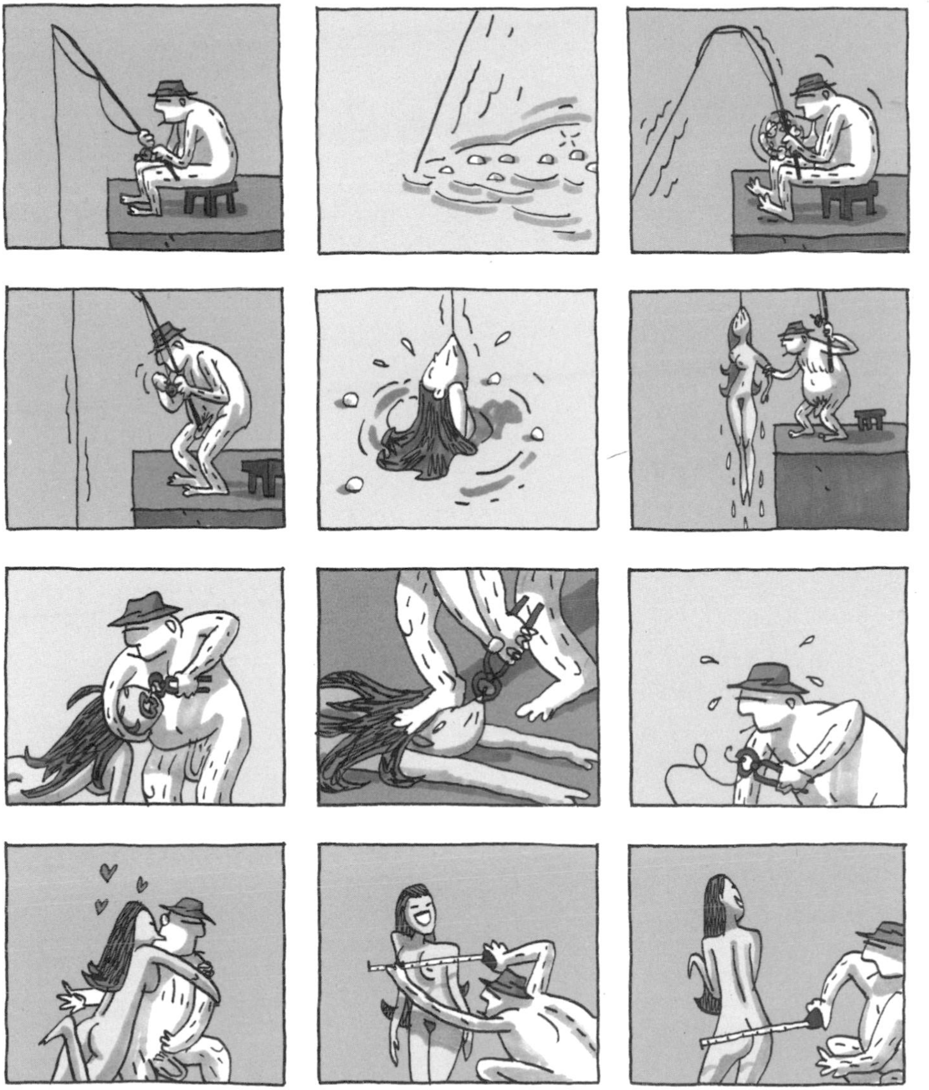
DELISLE

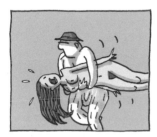

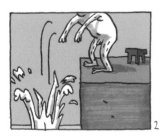

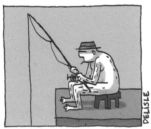

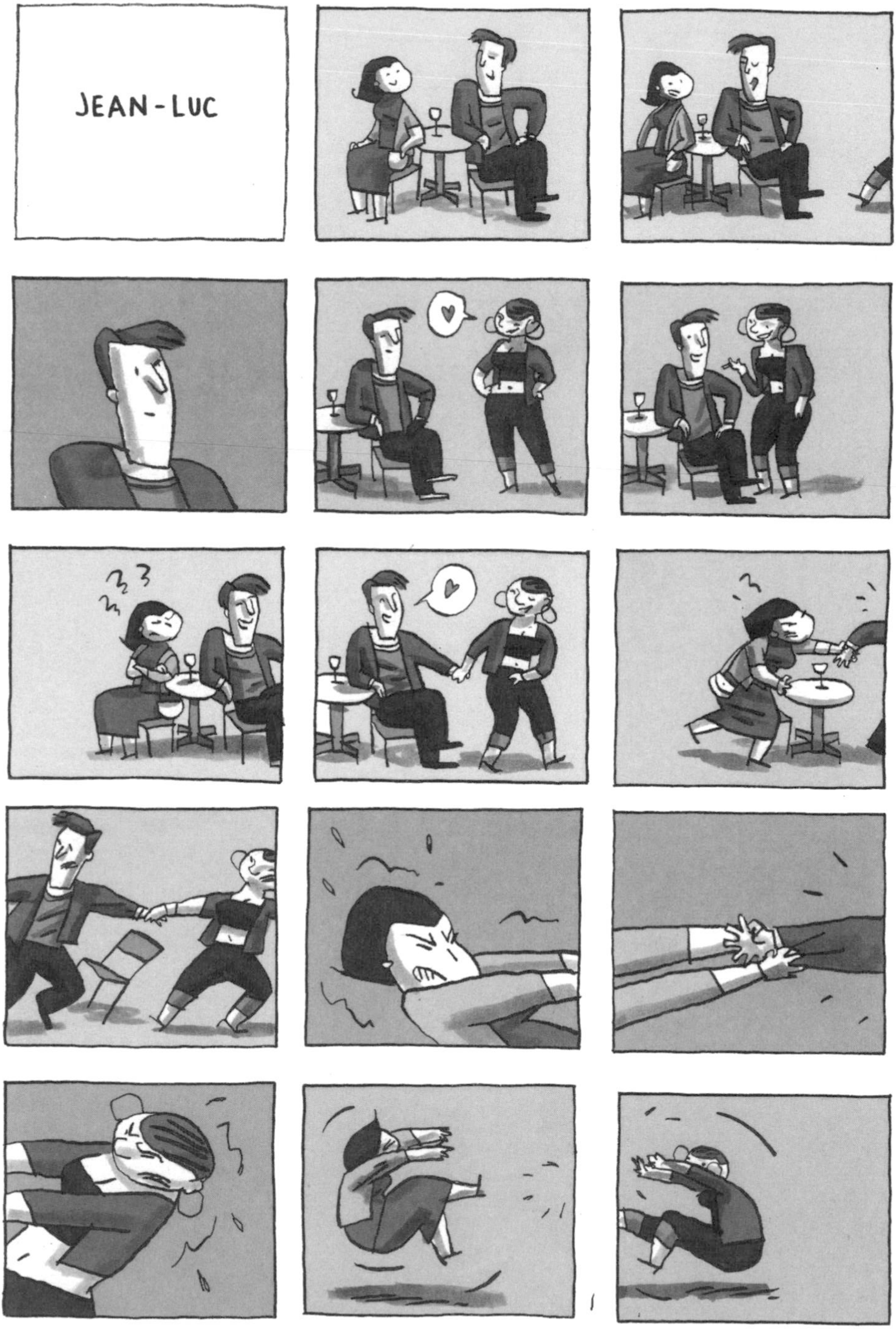
JEAN-LUC

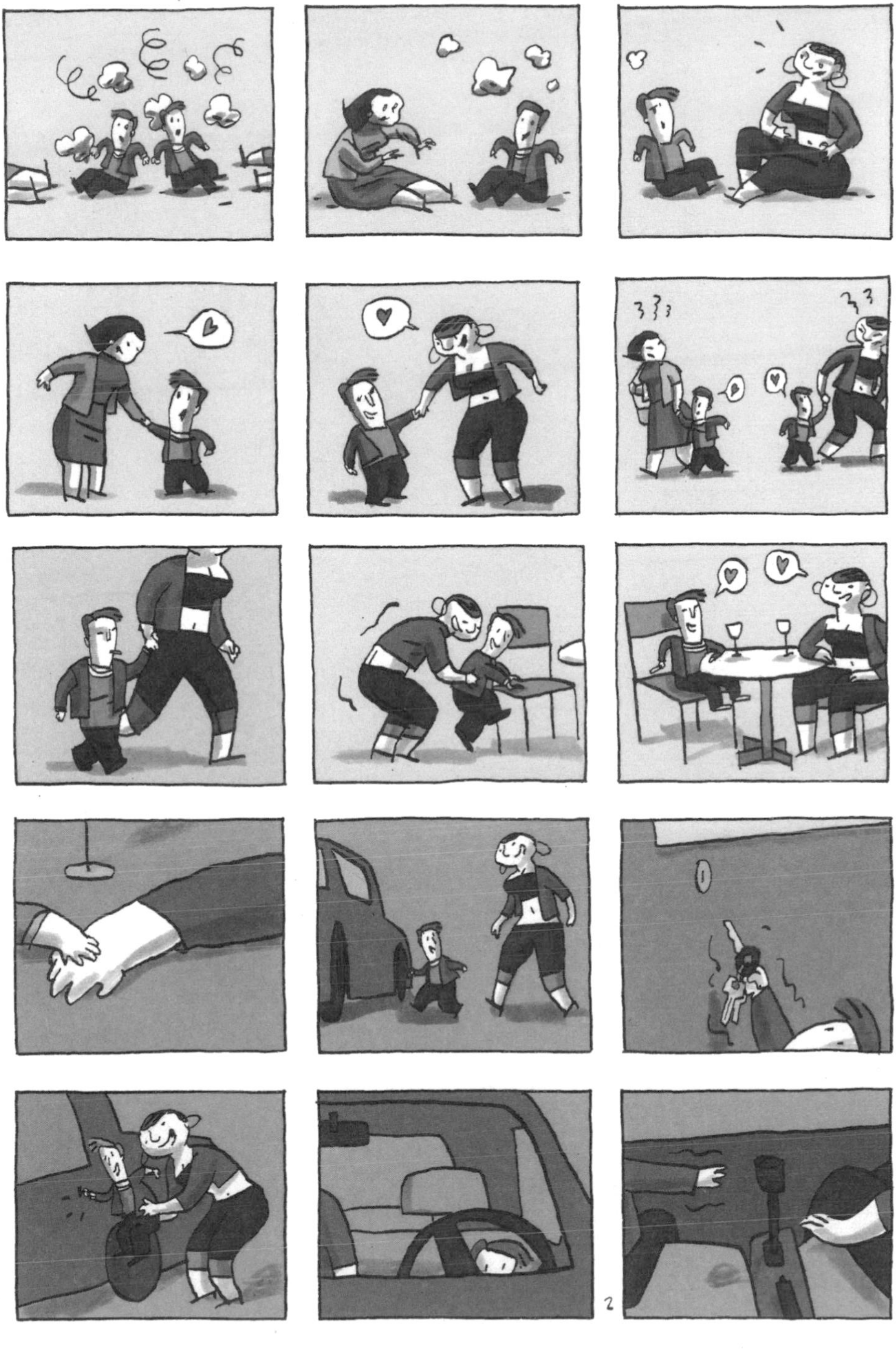

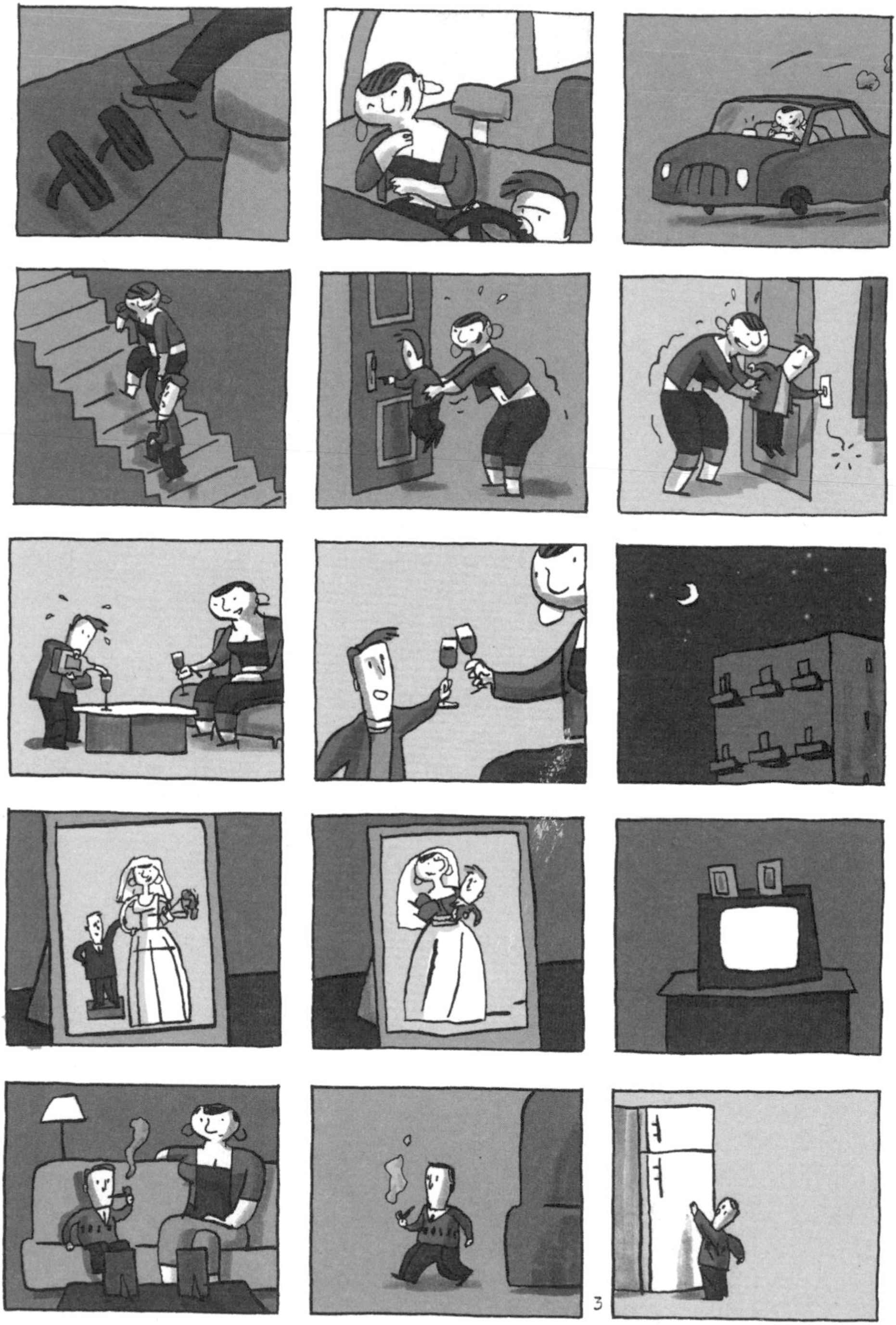

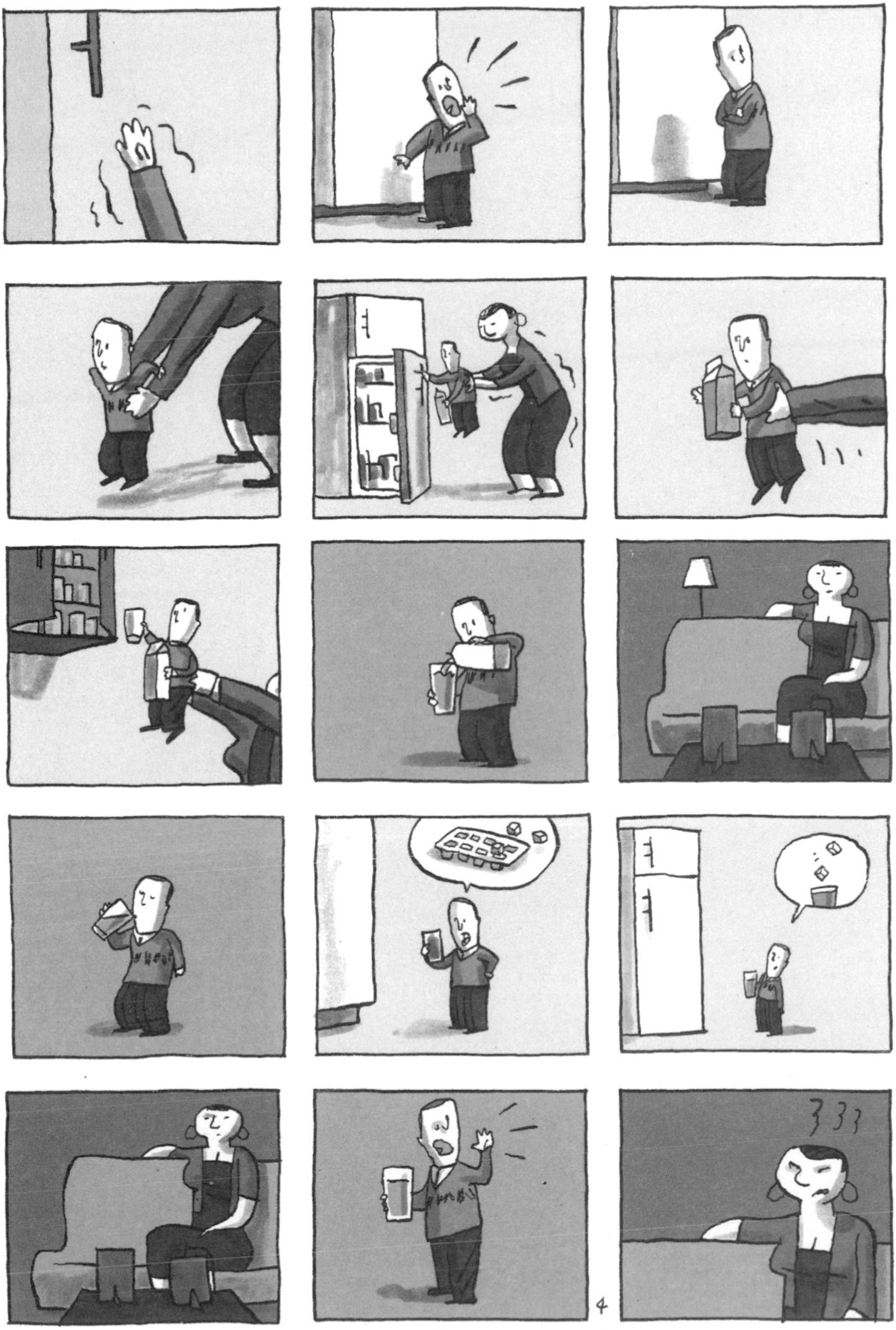

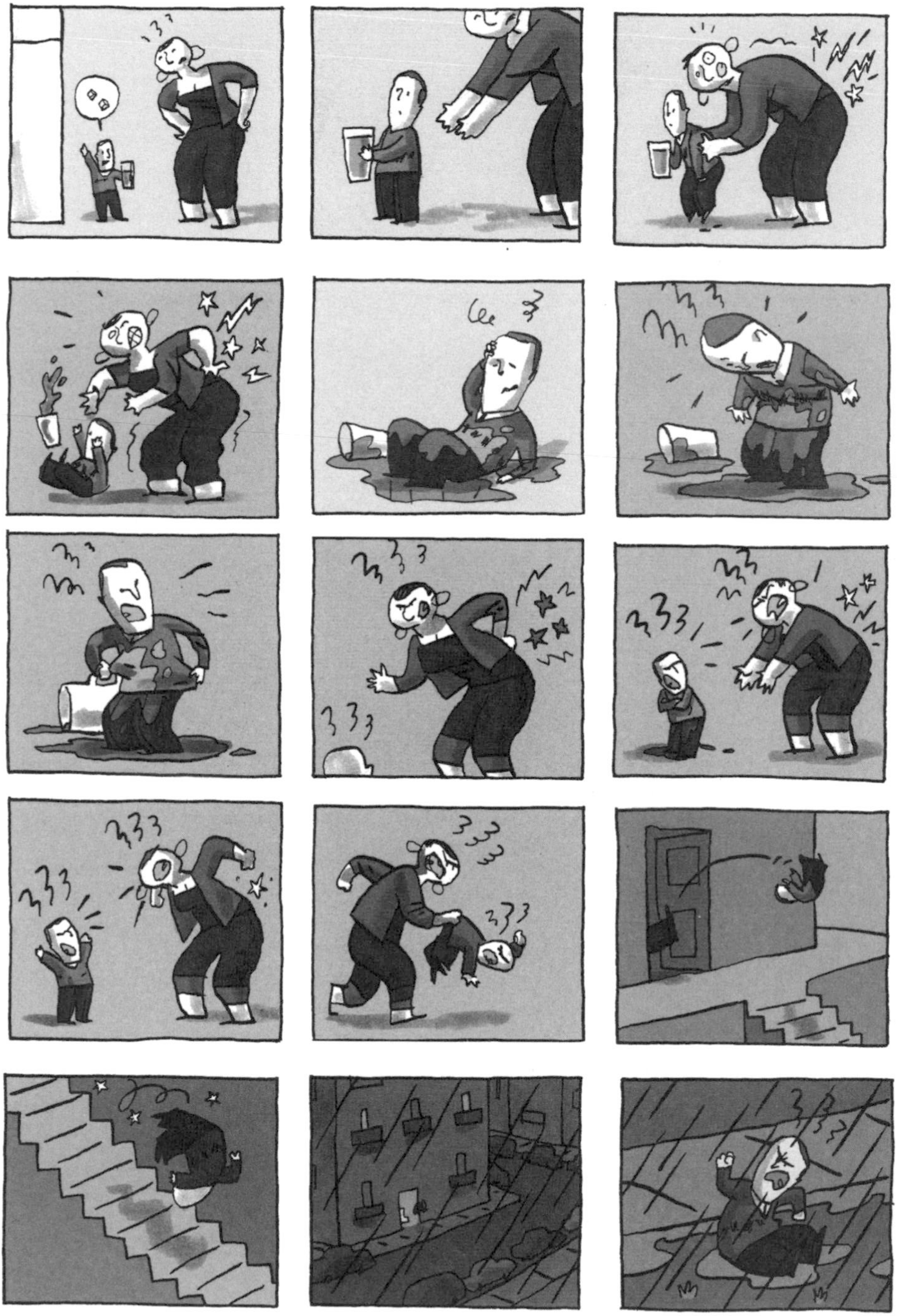

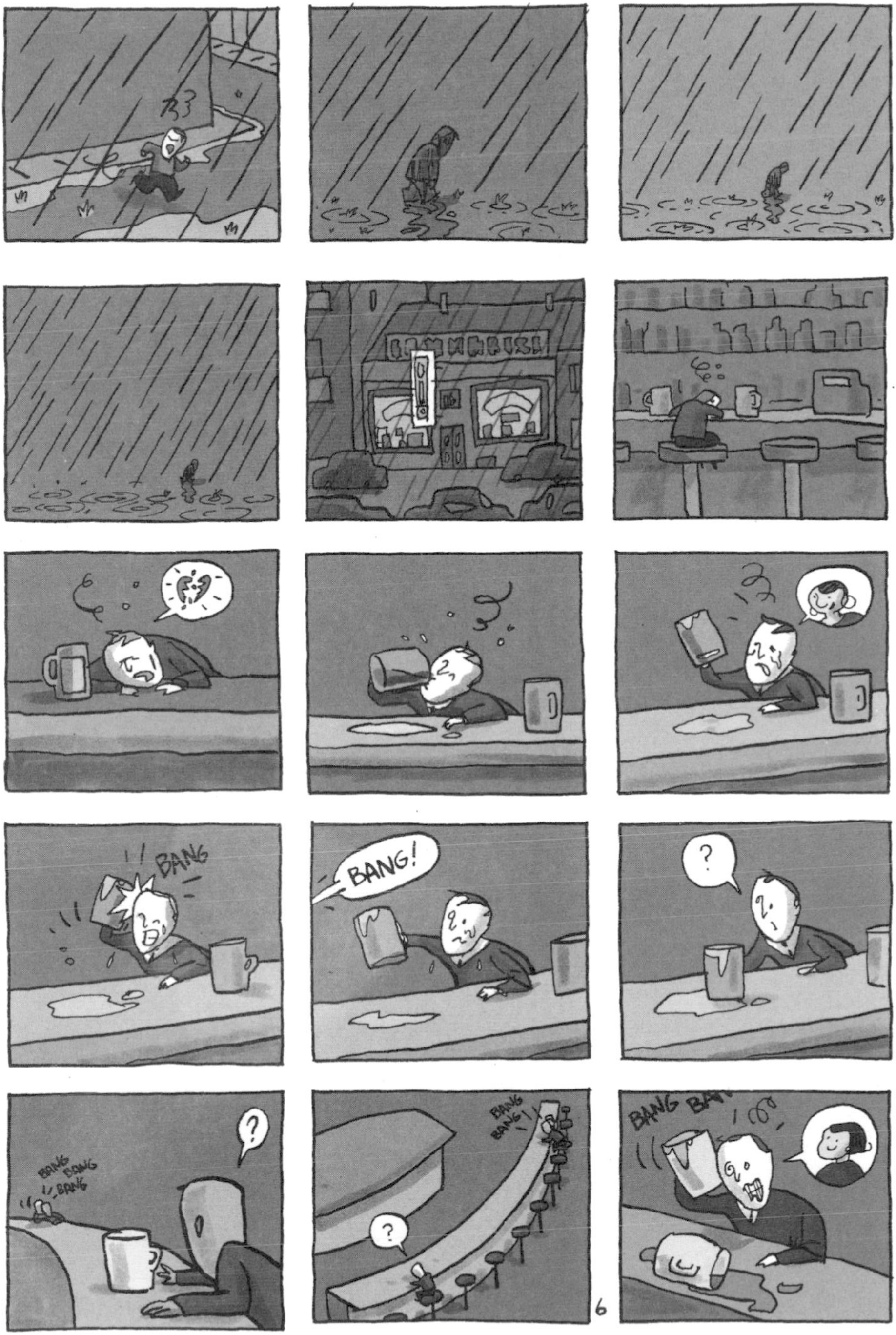
BANG
BANG!
?
BANG BANG BANG
?
BANG BANG
?
BANG BAN

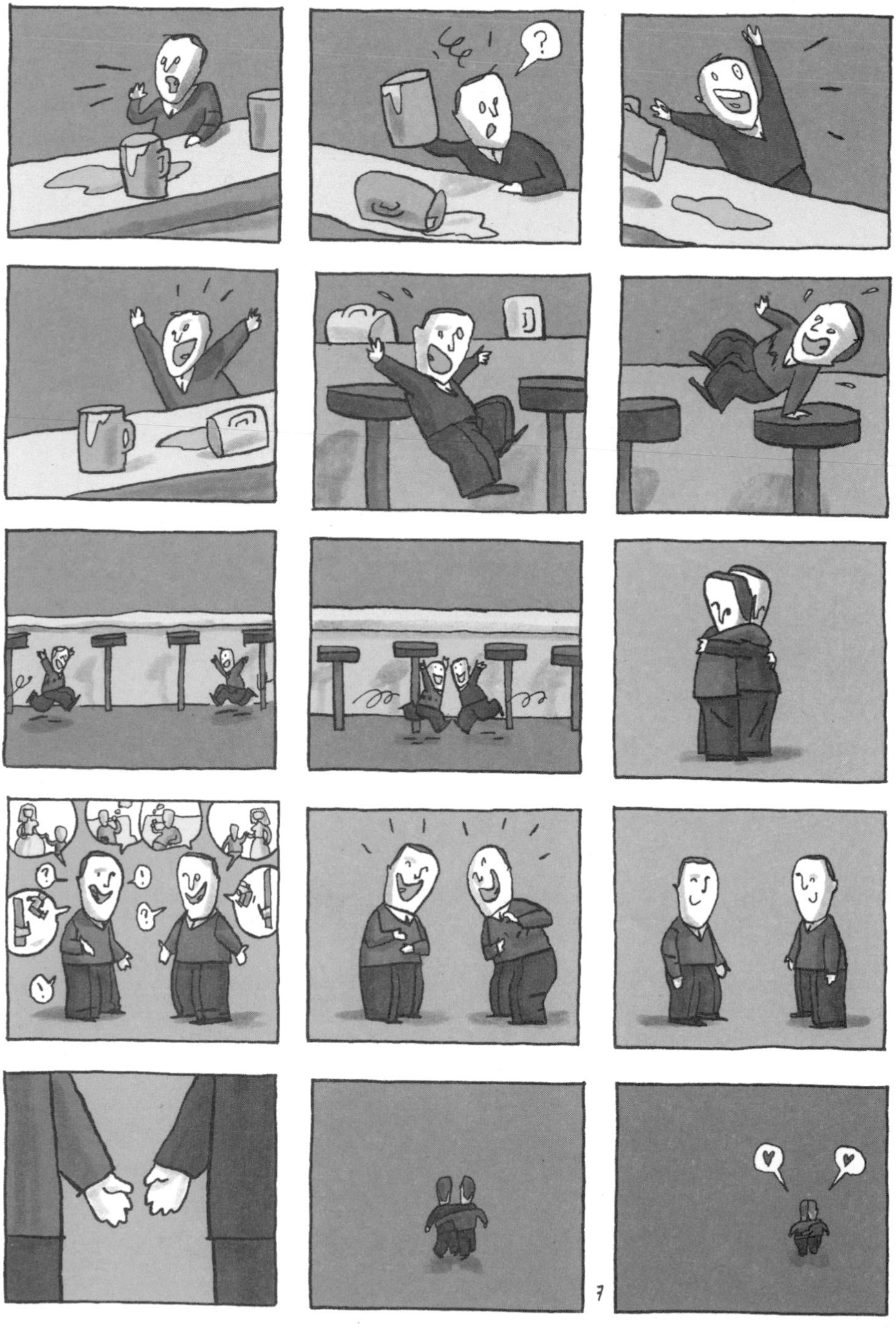
?
?
!
?
!

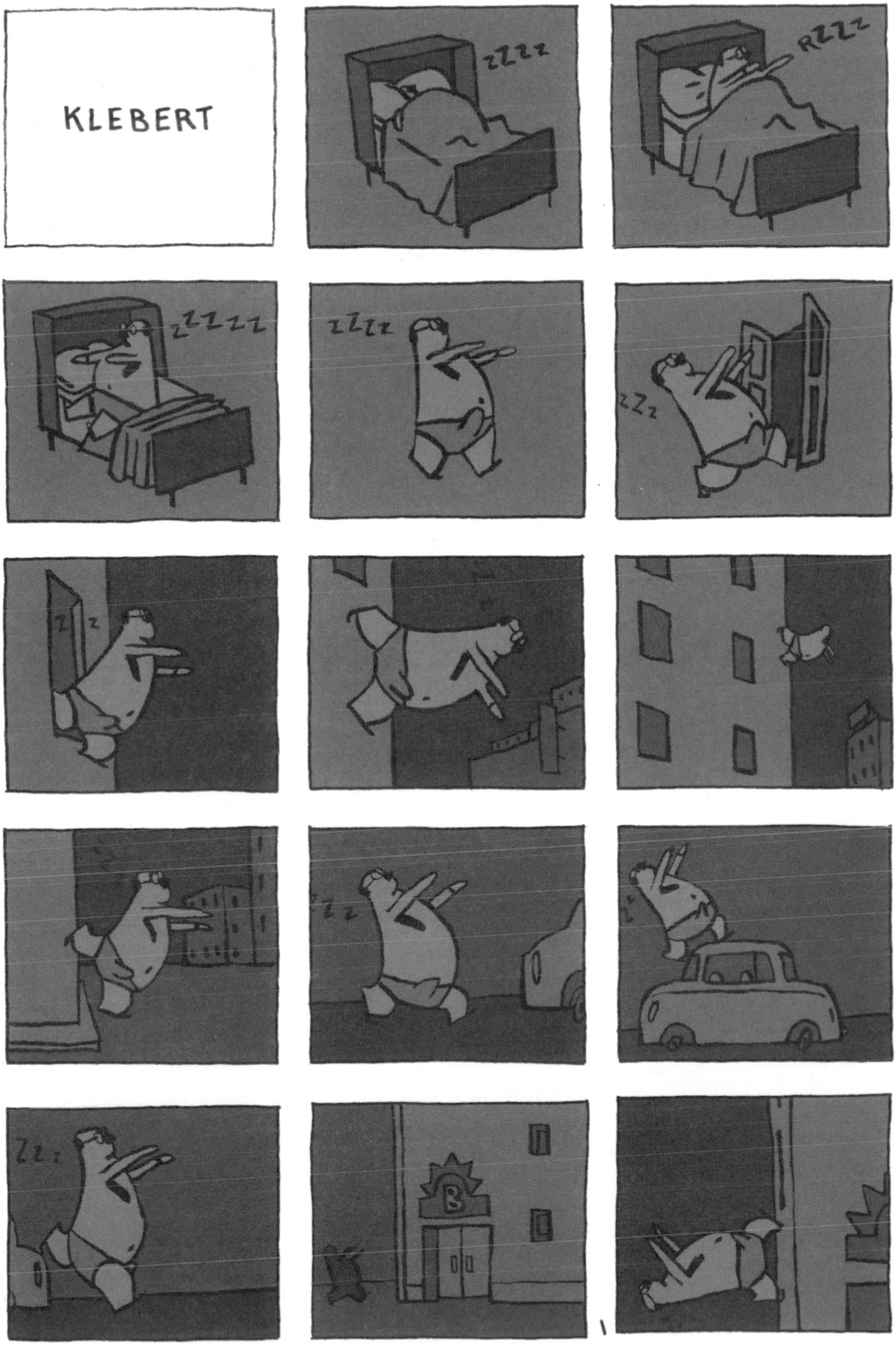
KLEBERT
zZZz
RZZz
zZZzz
zZzz
zZz
Zzz
B

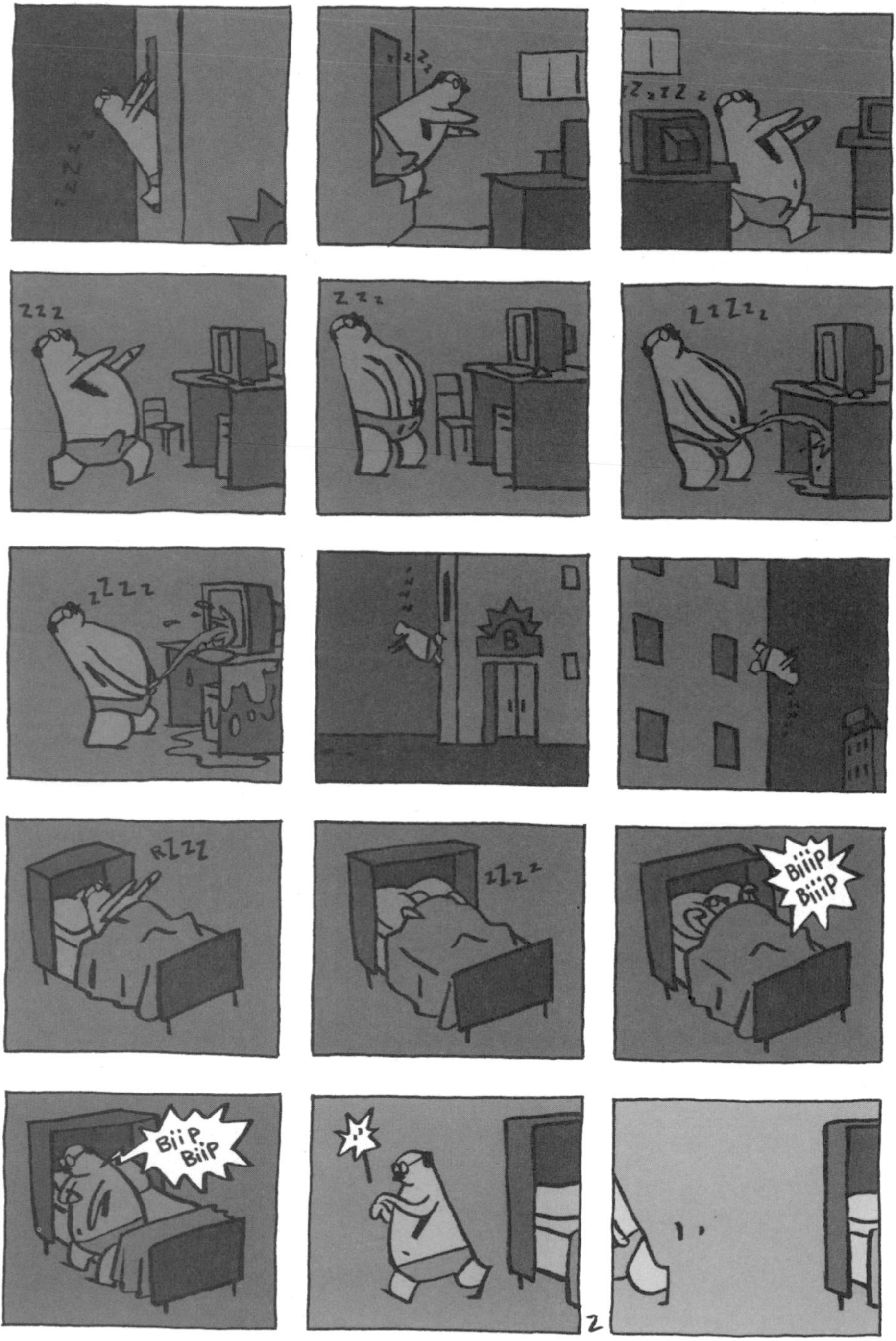
BiiiP BiiiP
BiiP. BiiP

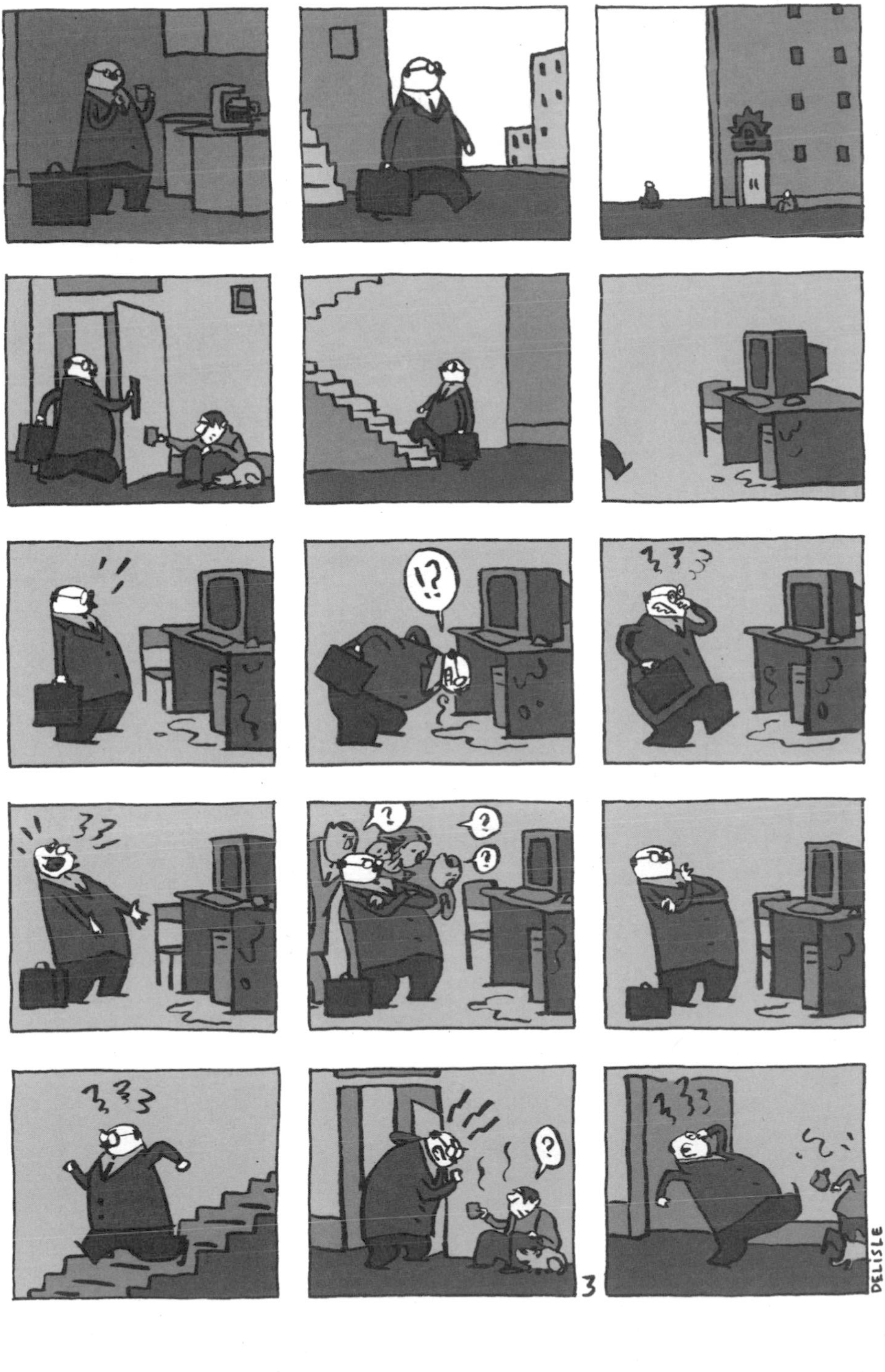
!?
?
?
?
?
DELISLE

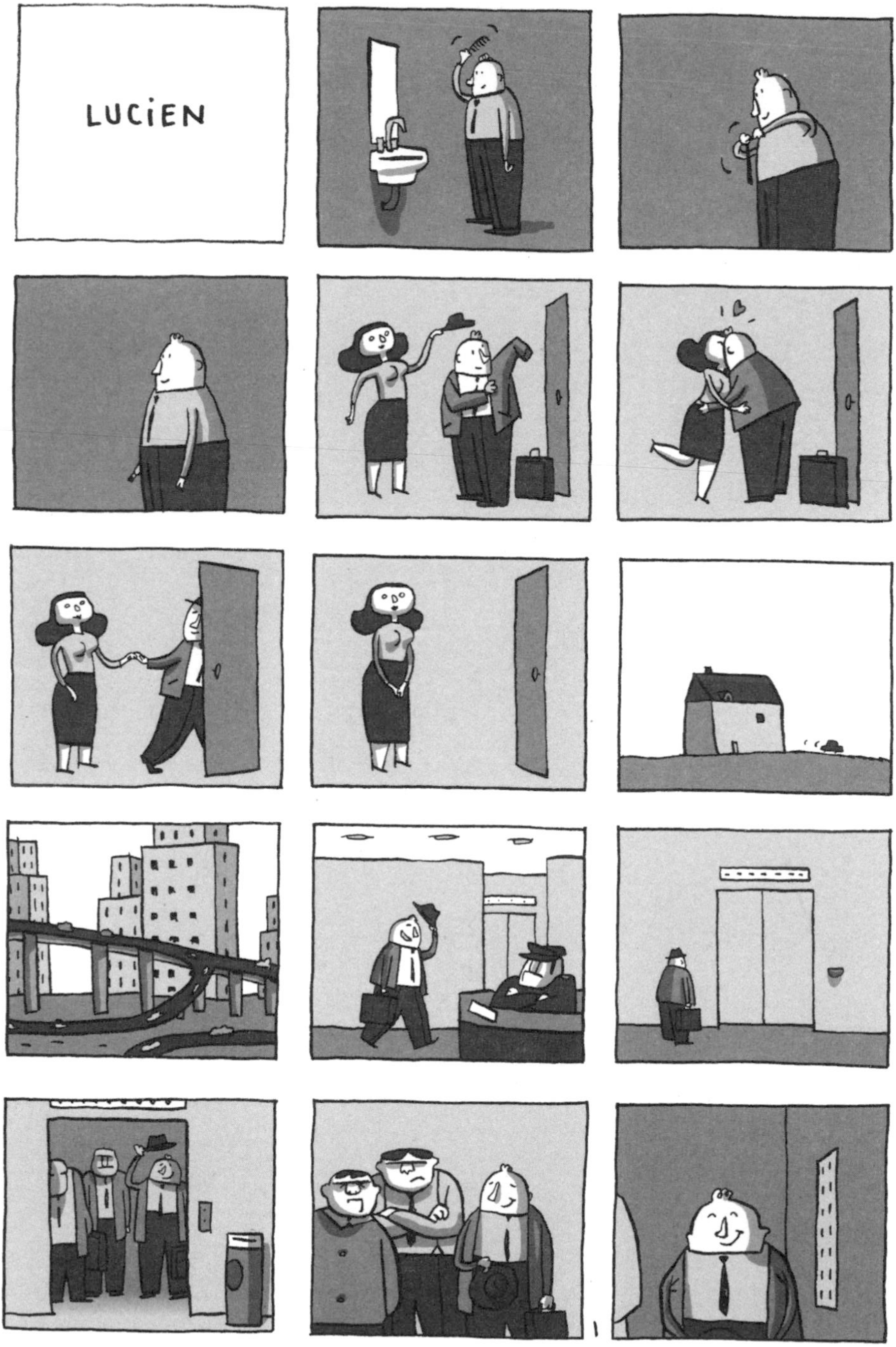
LUCiEN

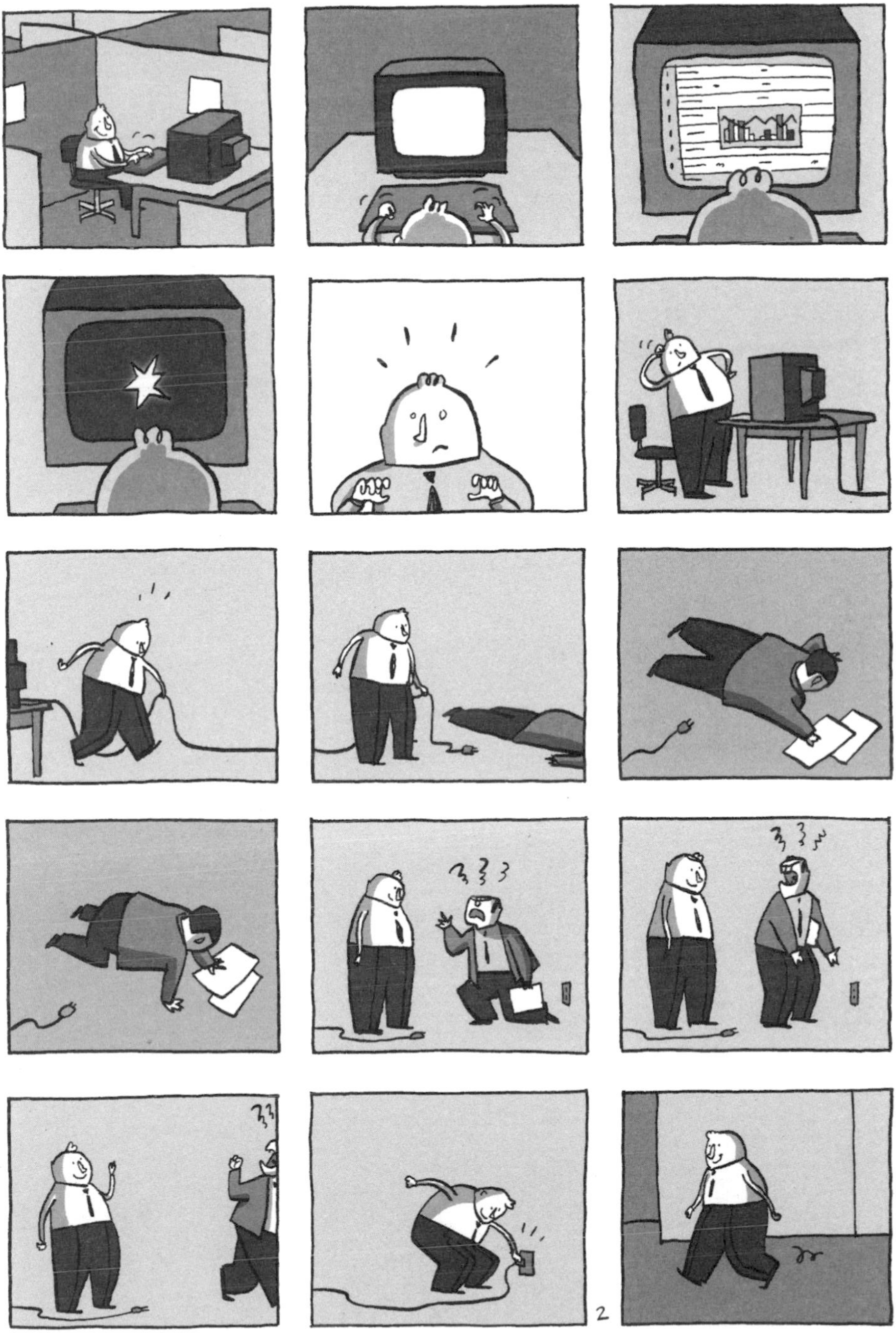

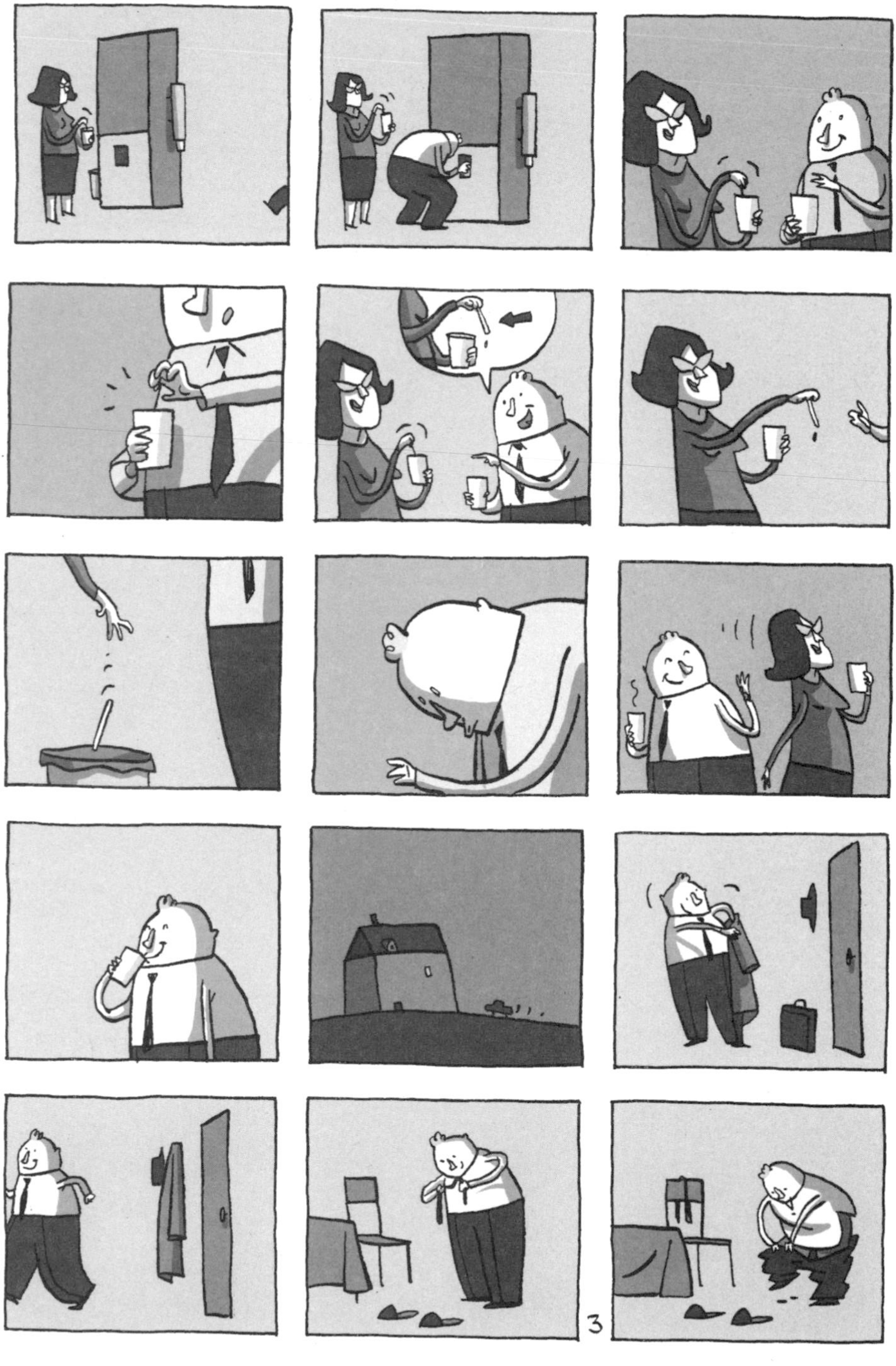

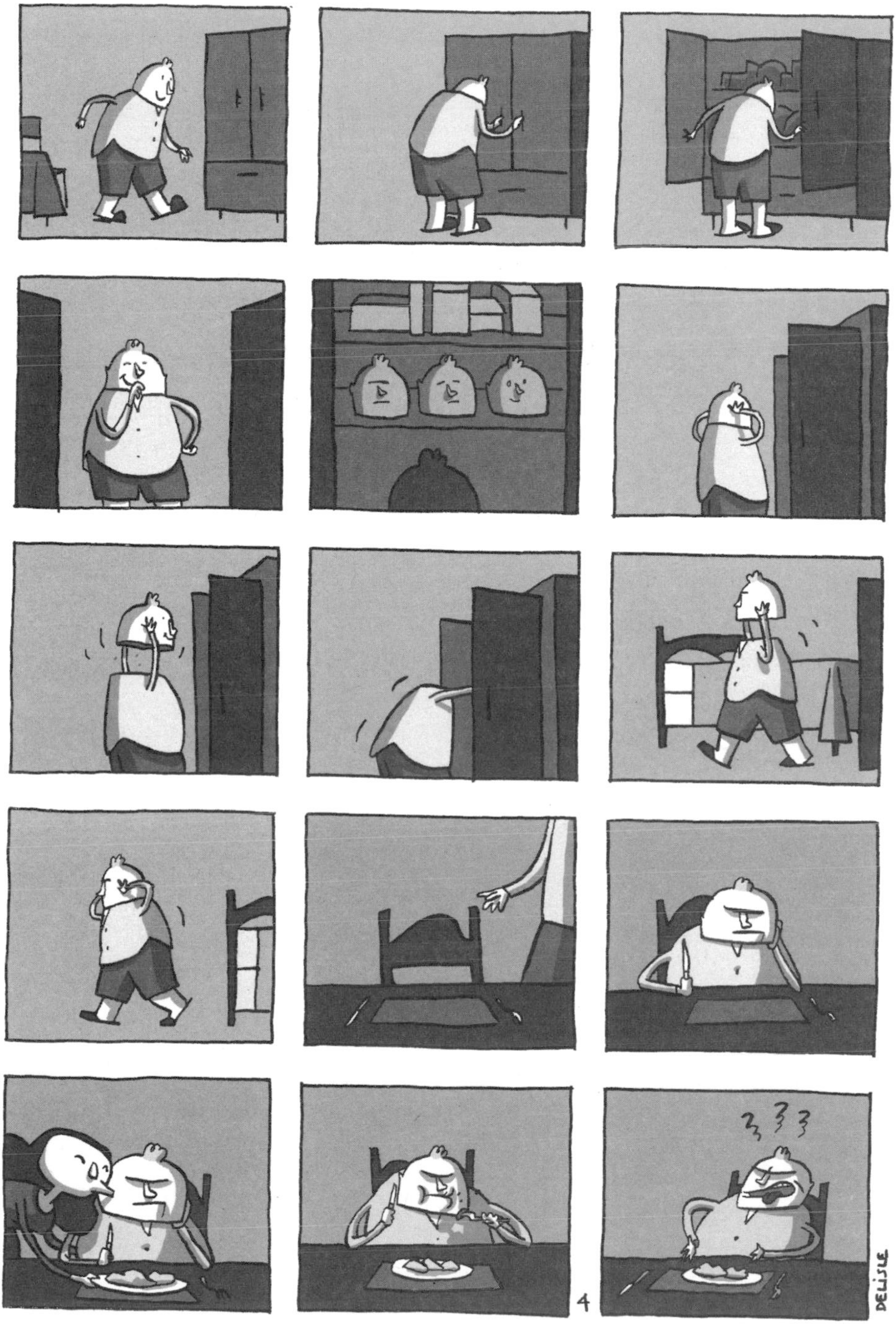

DELISLE

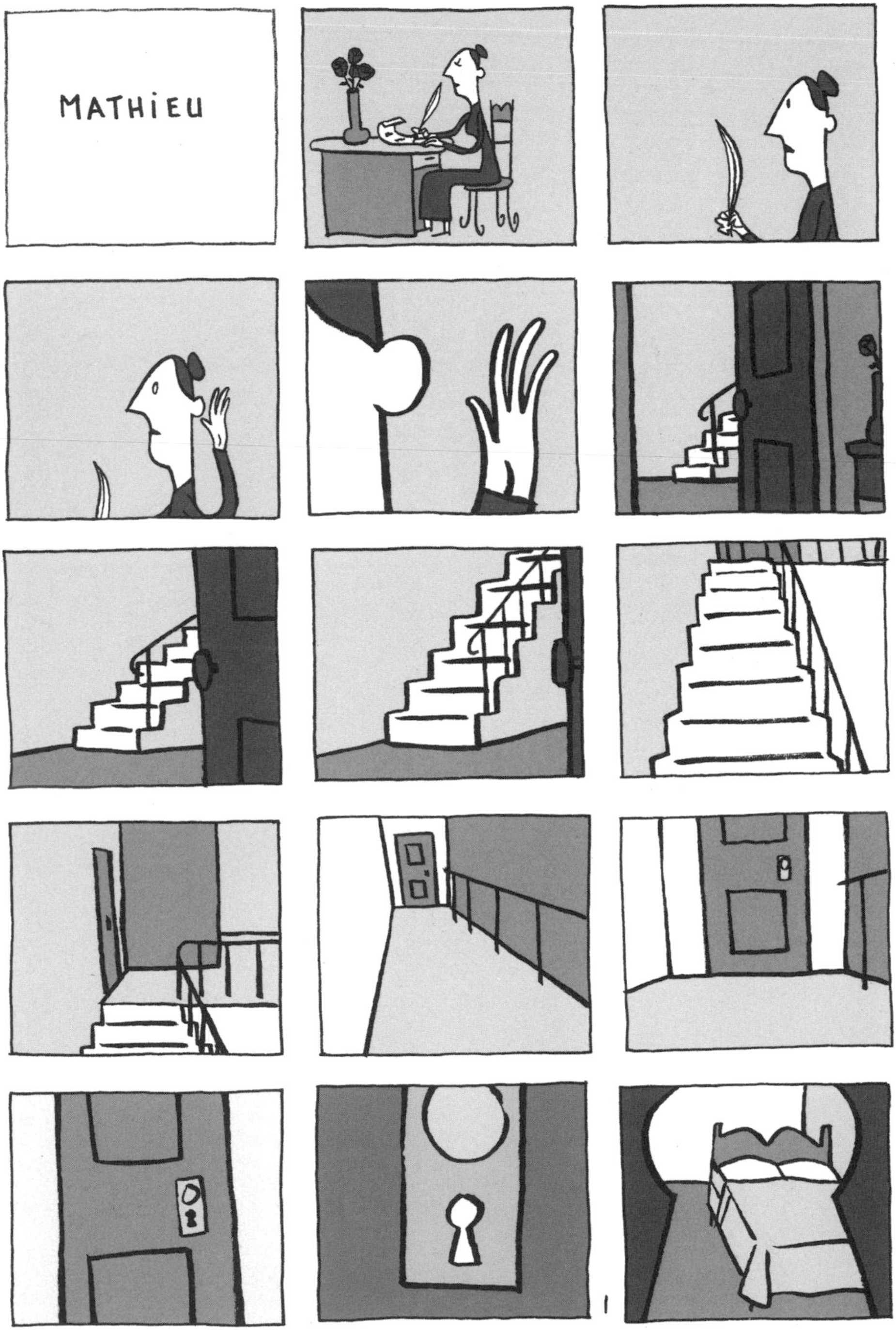
MATHIEU

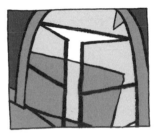

2

DELISLE

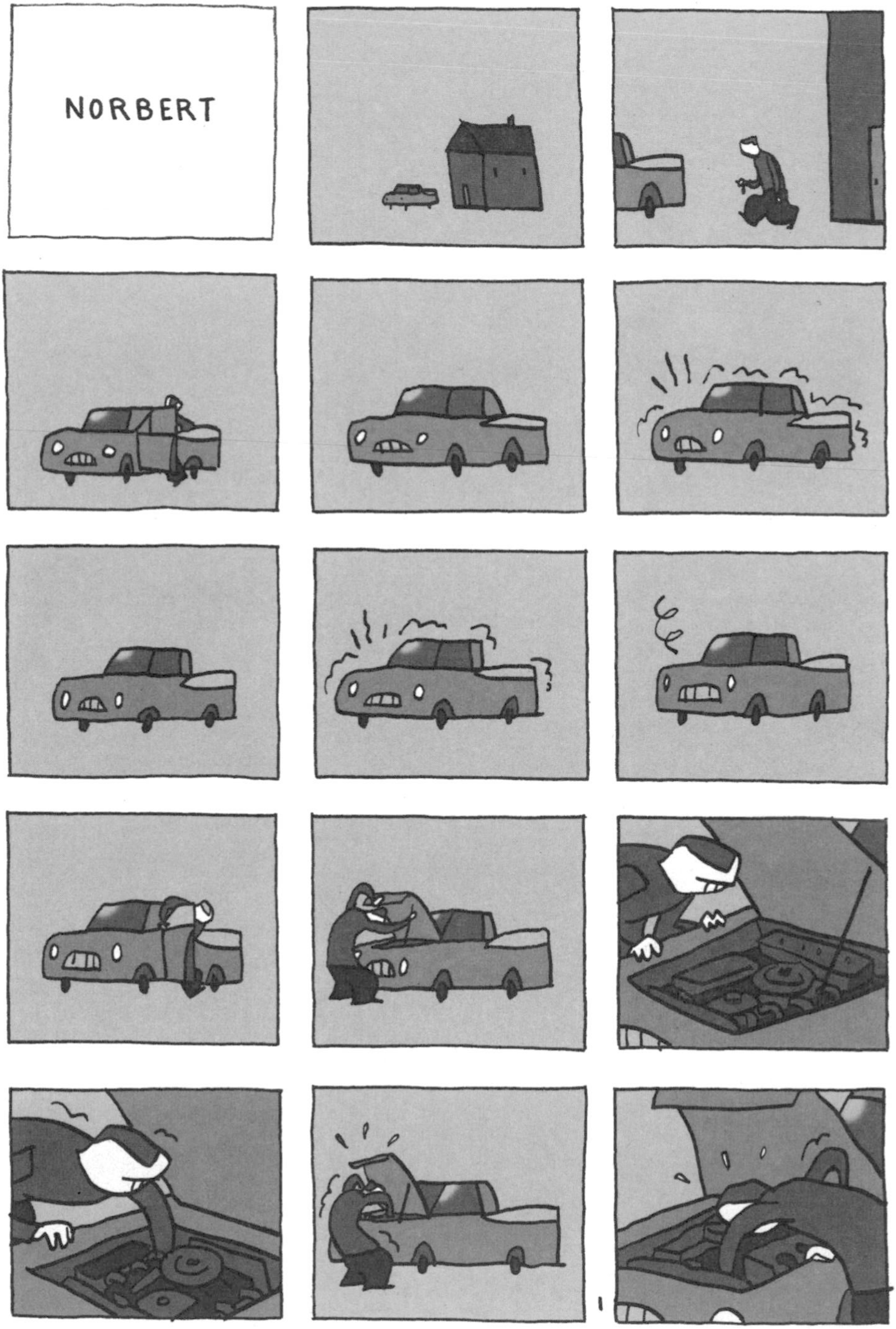
NORBERT

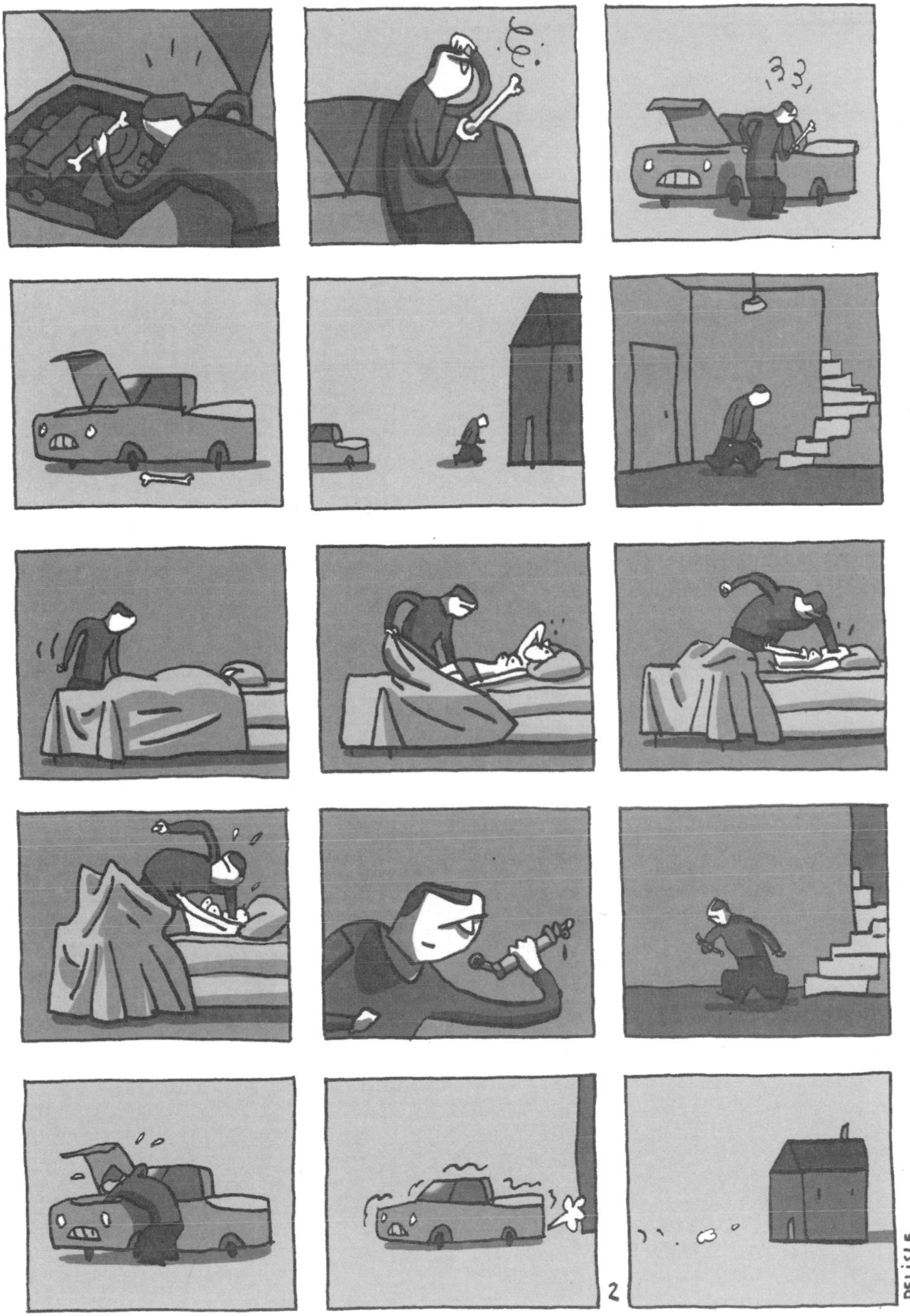
2
DELISLE

OLIVIER

1

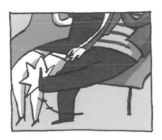

2

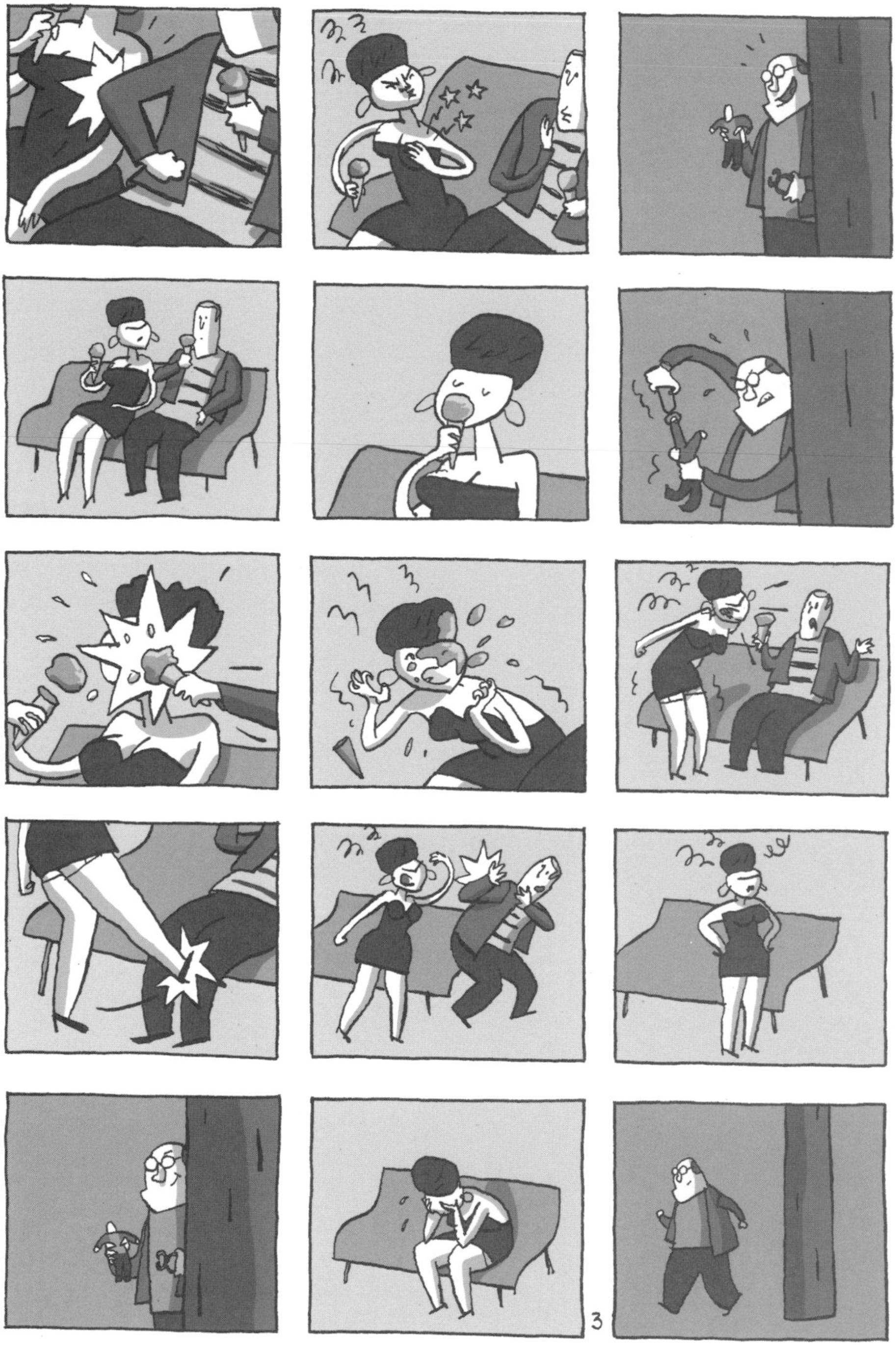

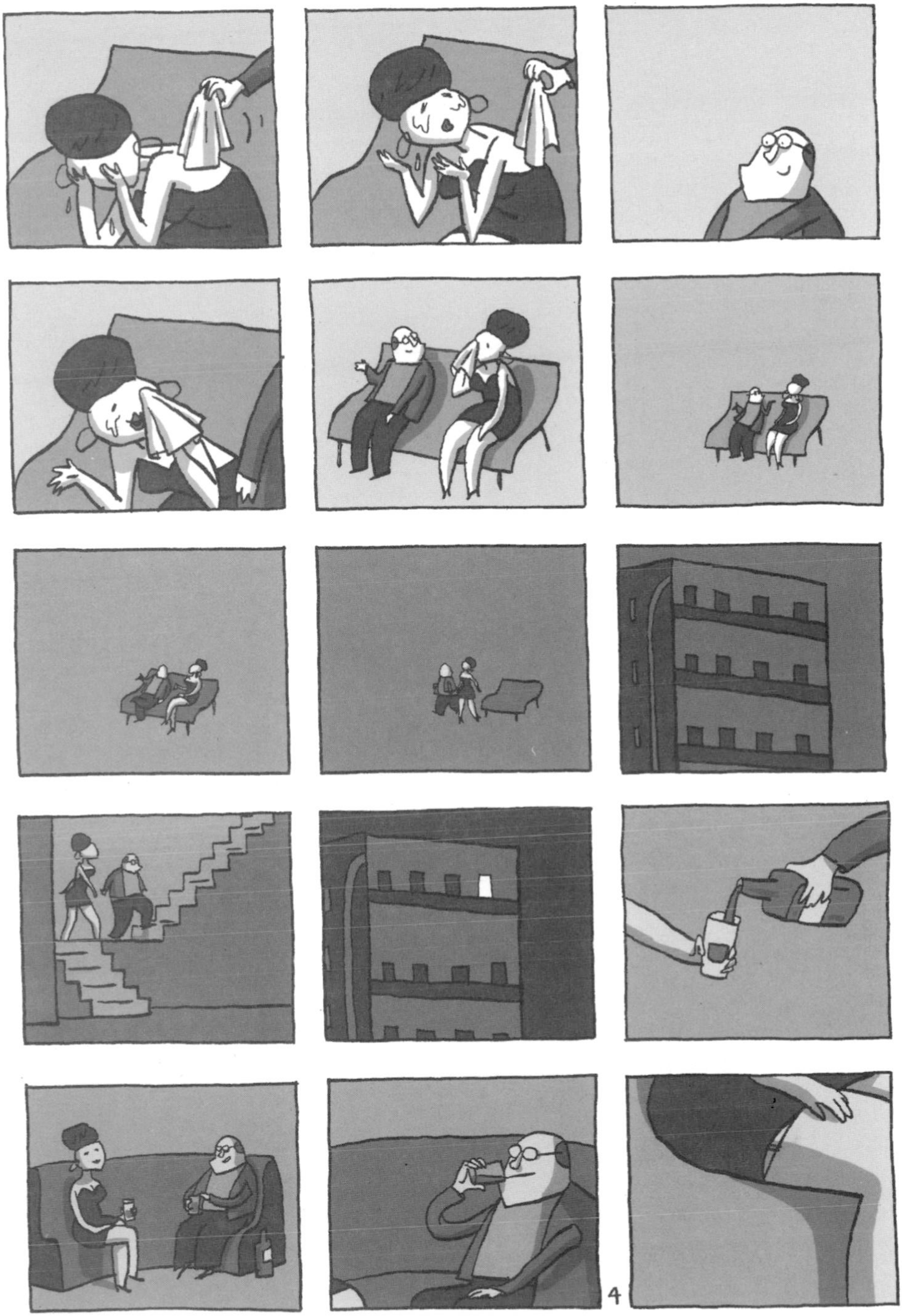

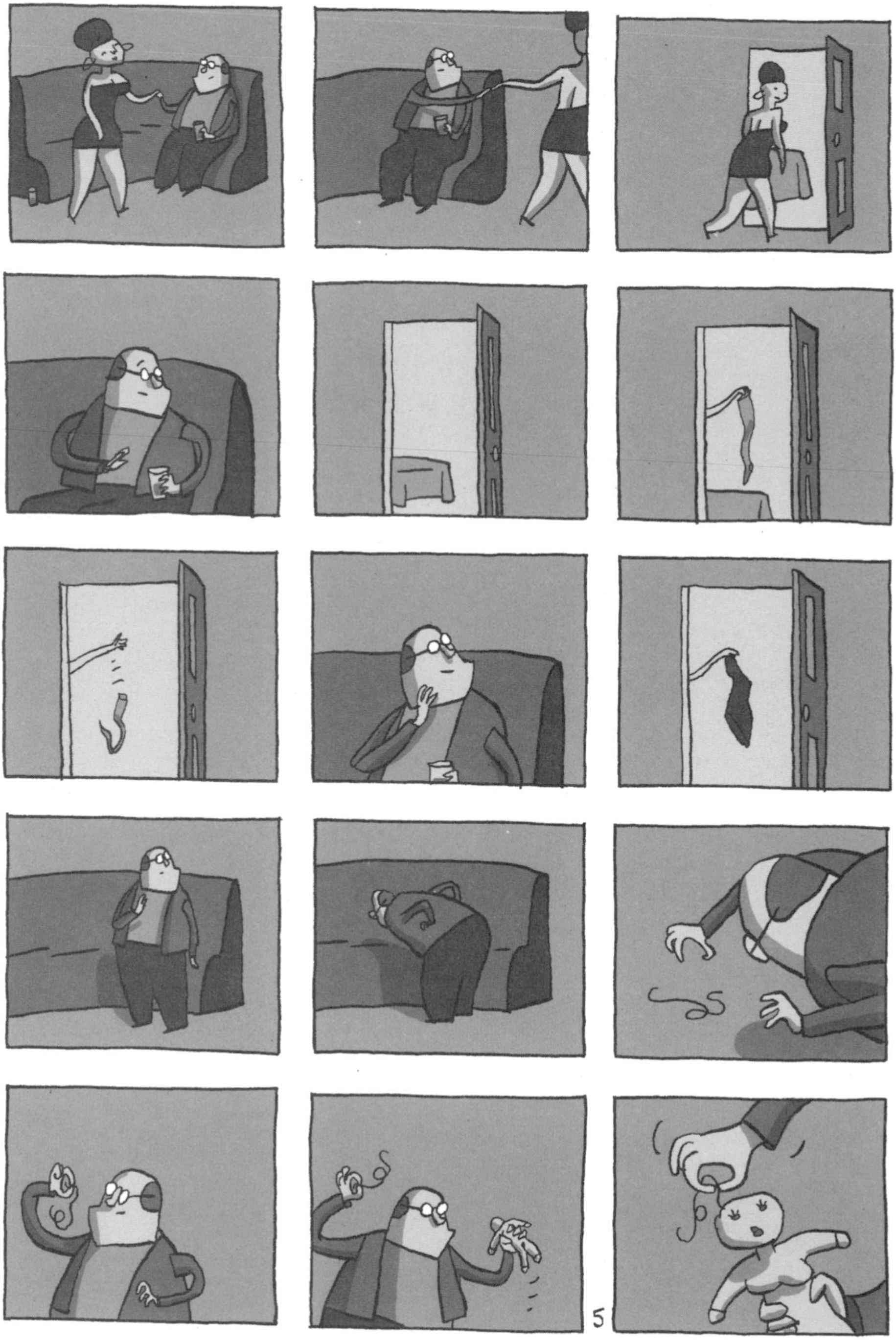

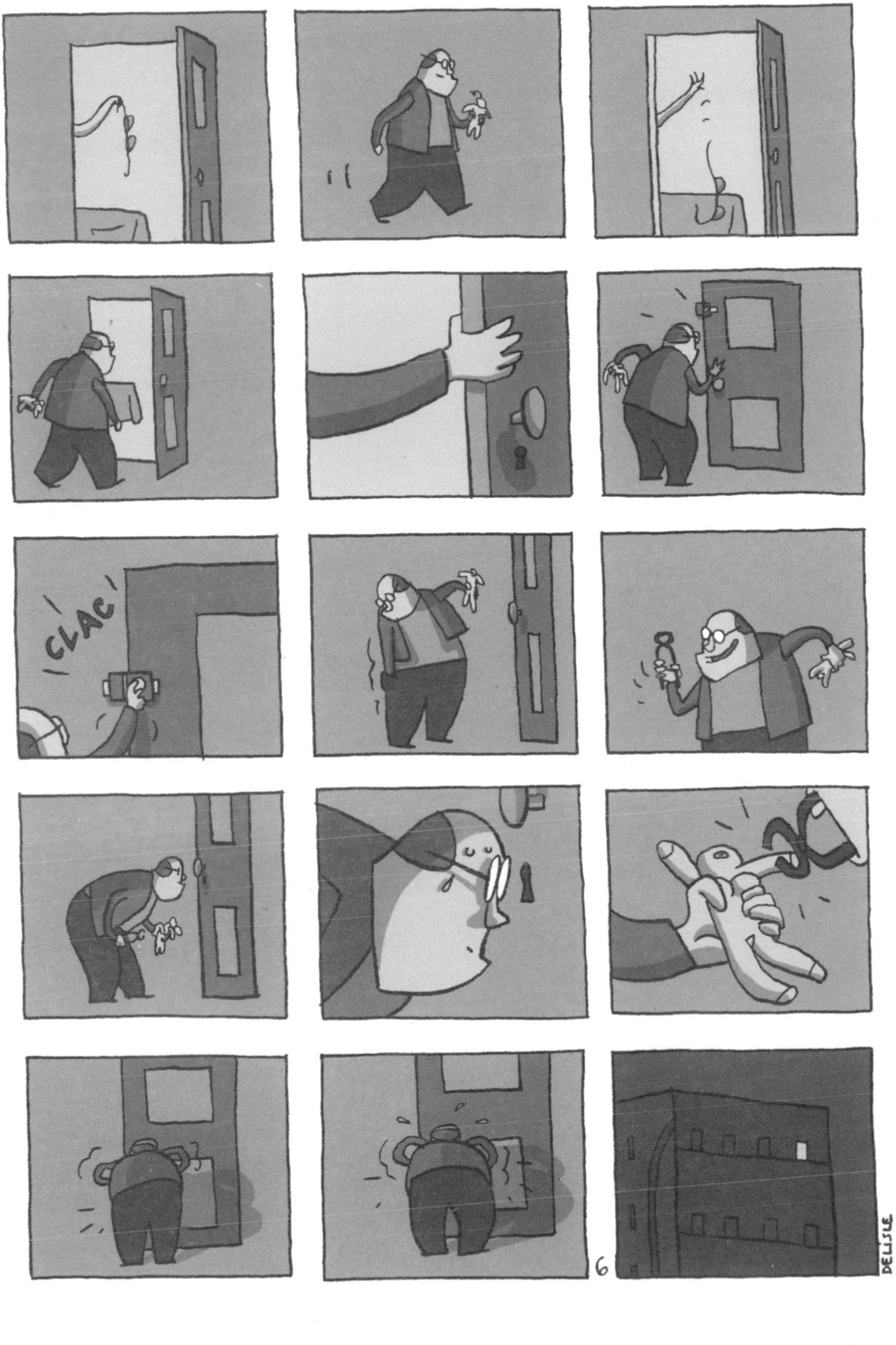
CLAC
DELISLE

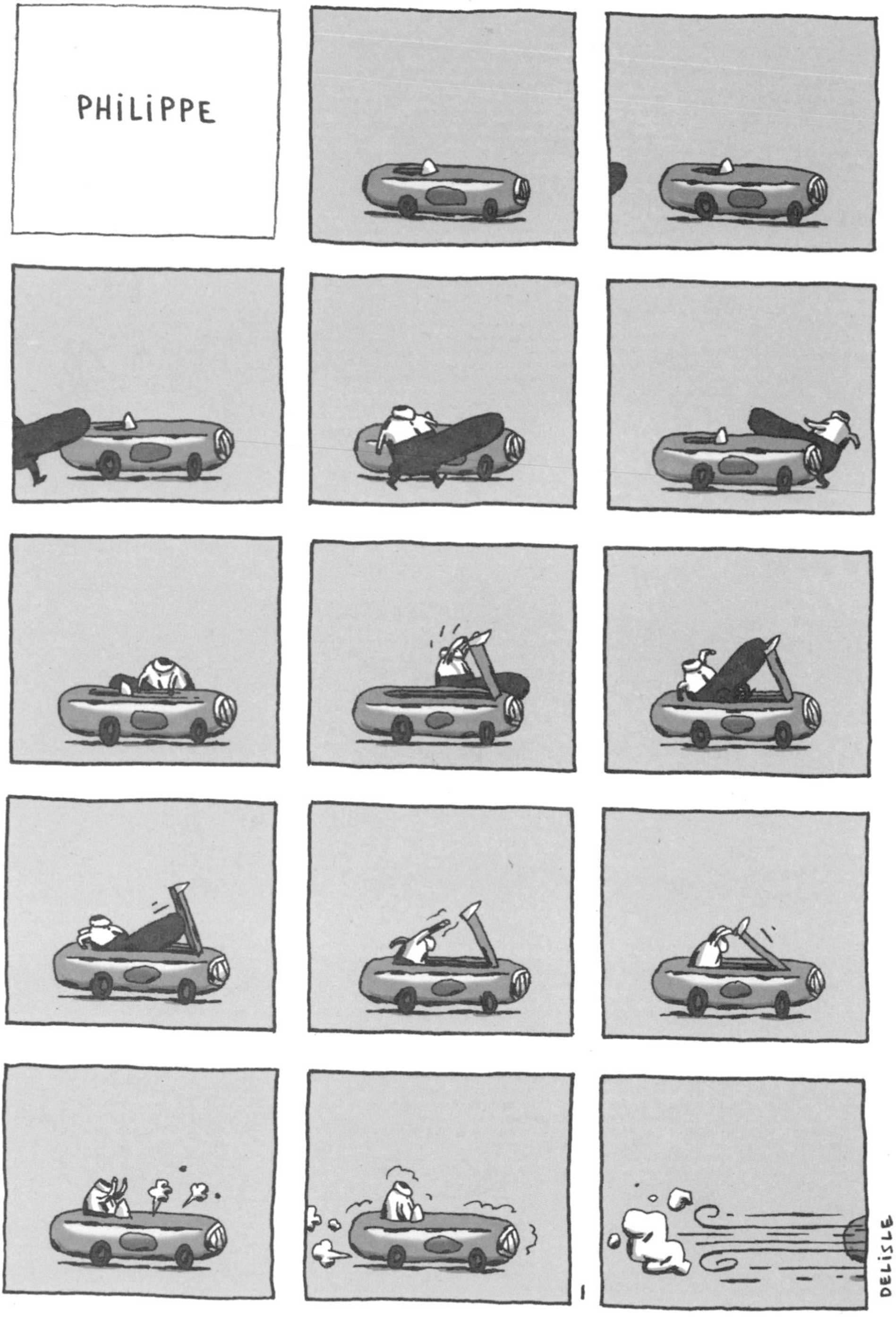
PHILIPPE
DELISLE

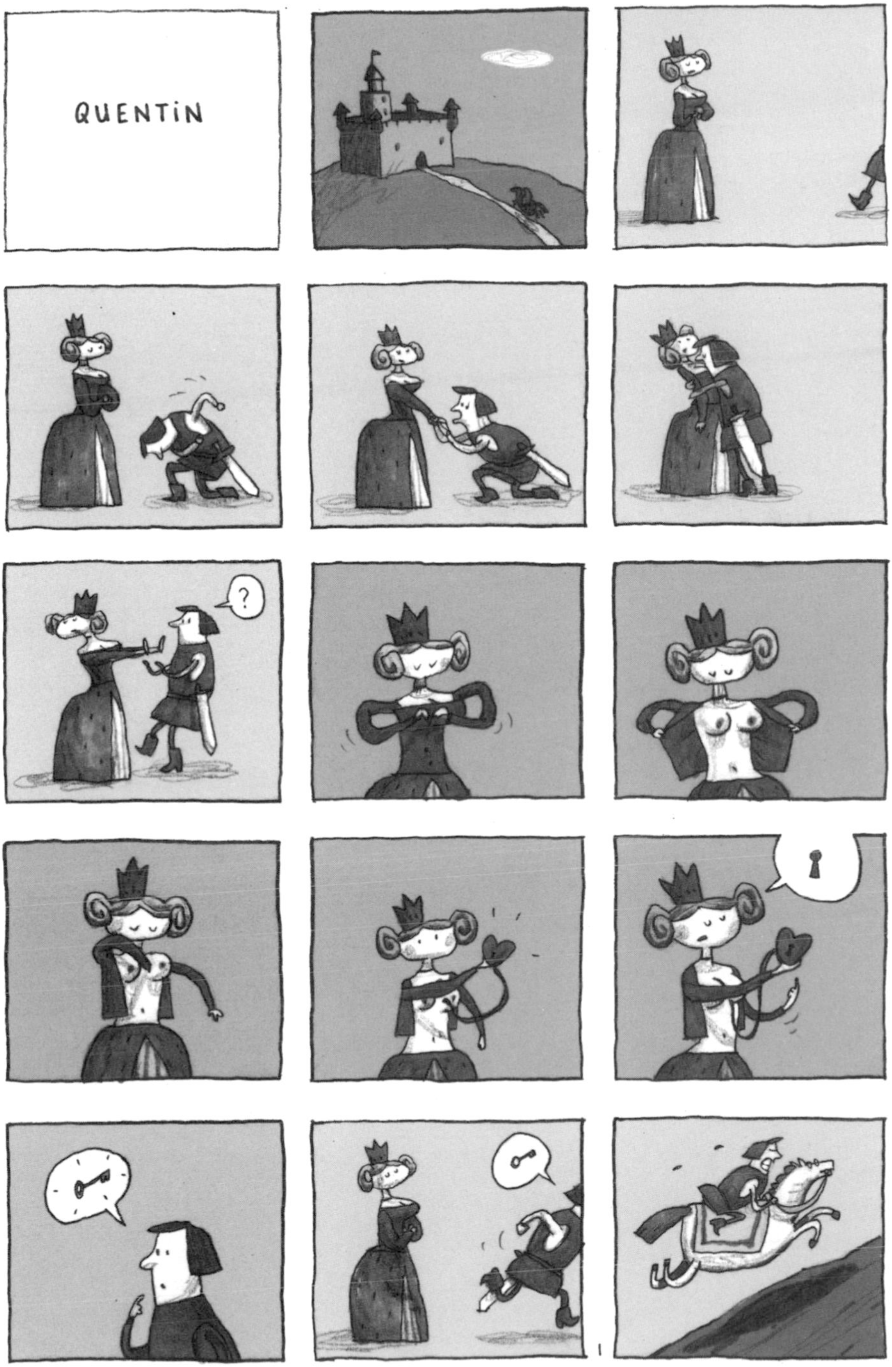
QUENTIN
?

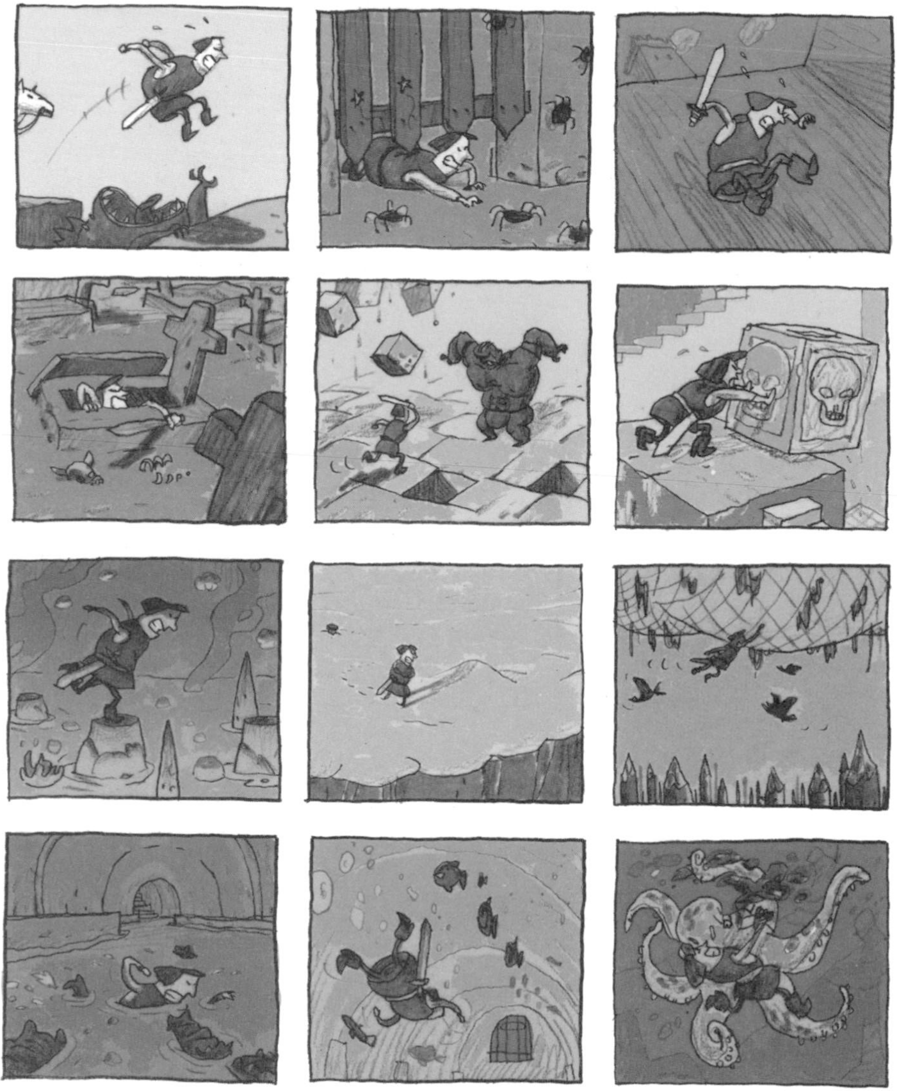

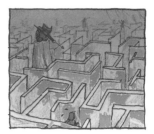

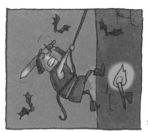

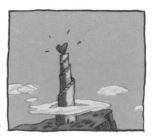

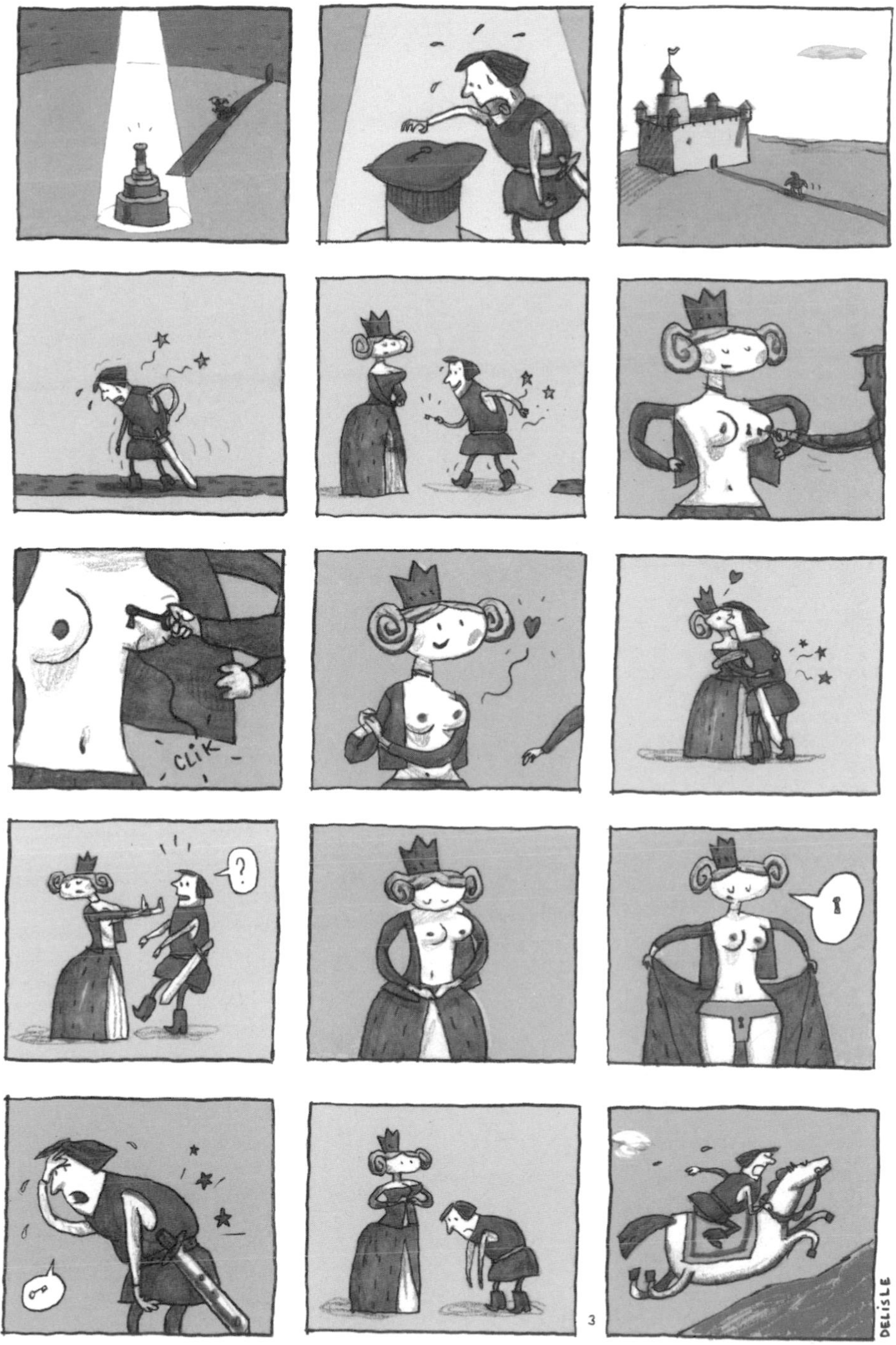
CLIK
?
DELISLE

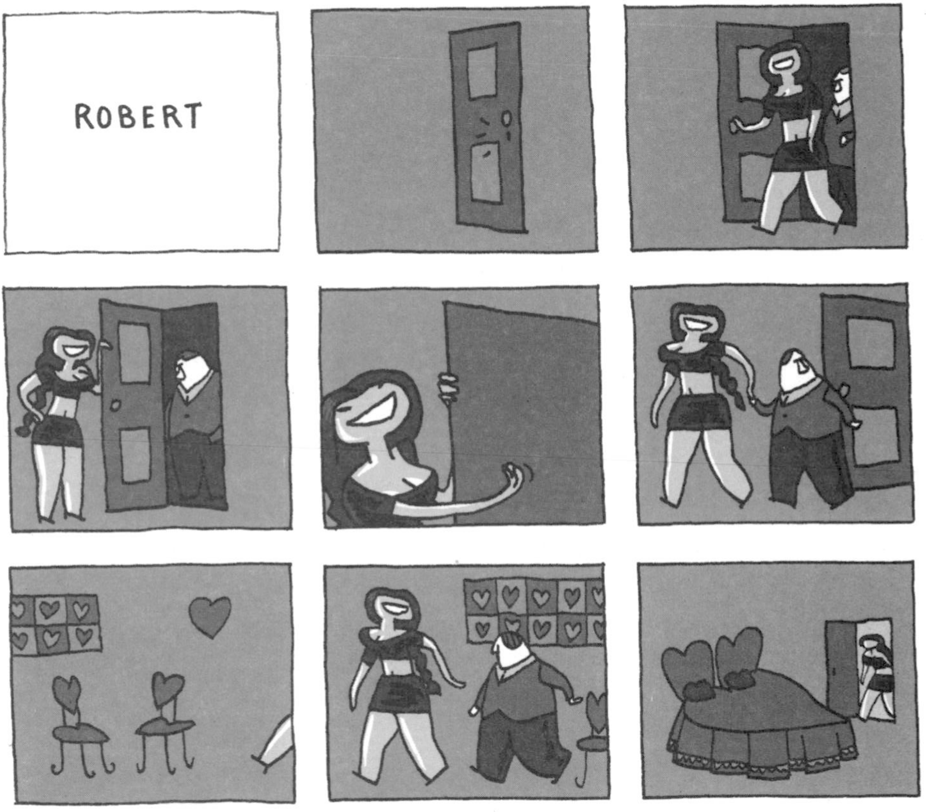
ROBERT
A
B
A

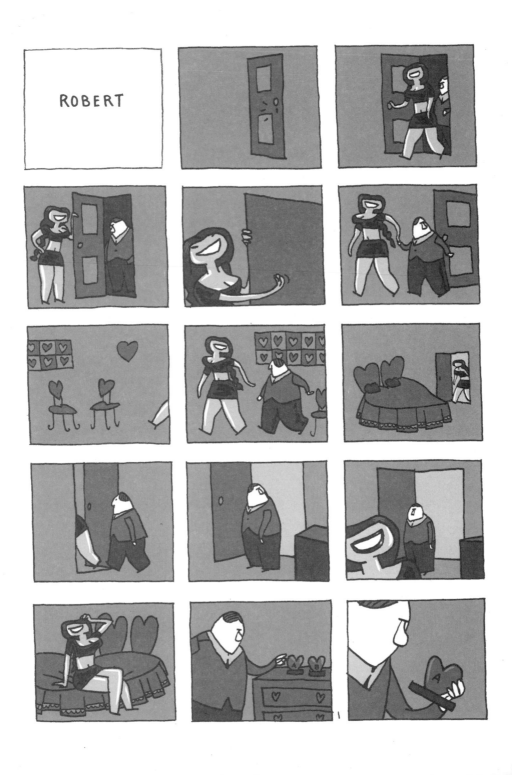

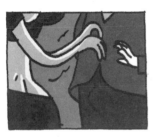  

 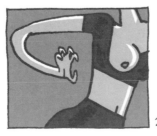 

2

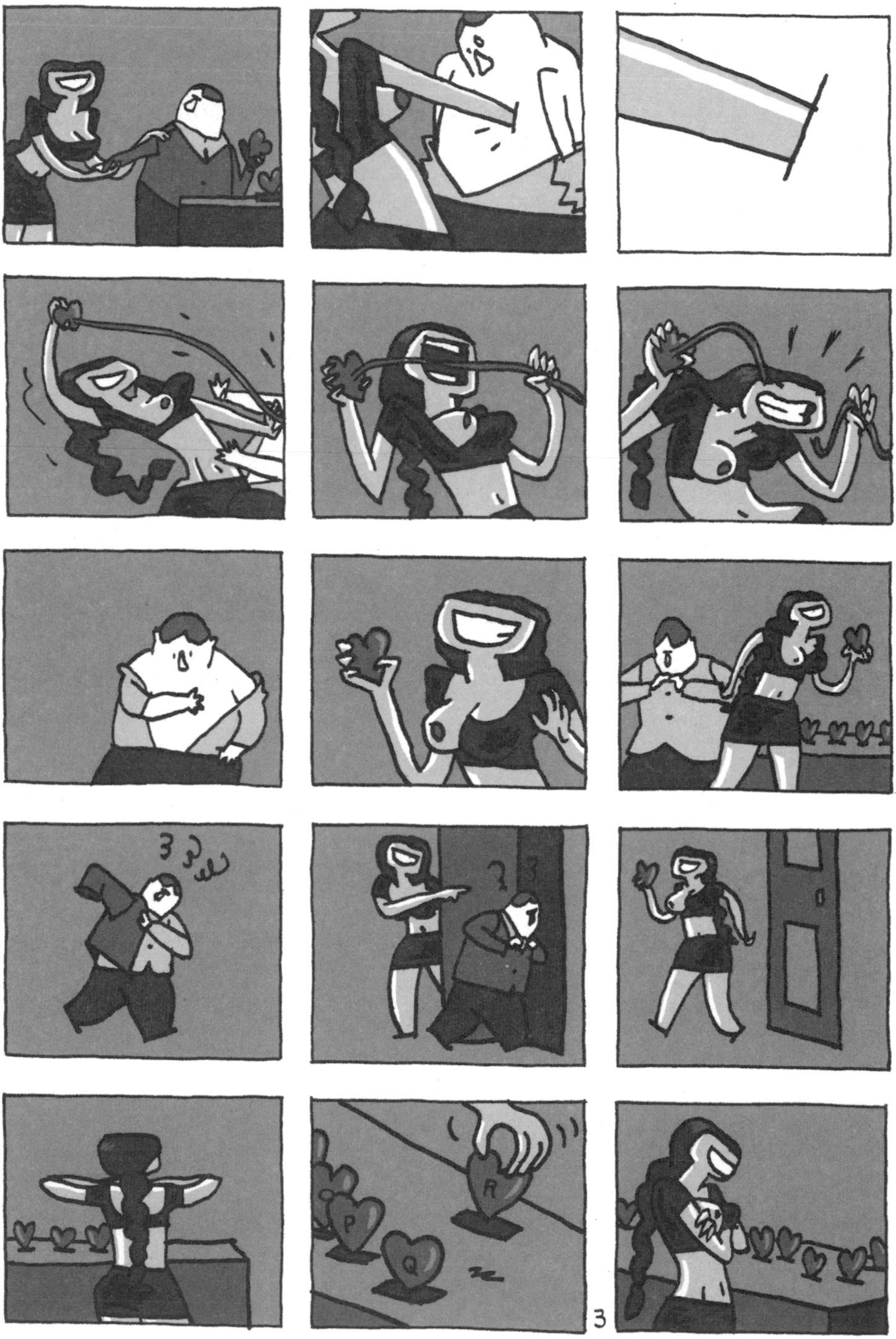
R
P
Q

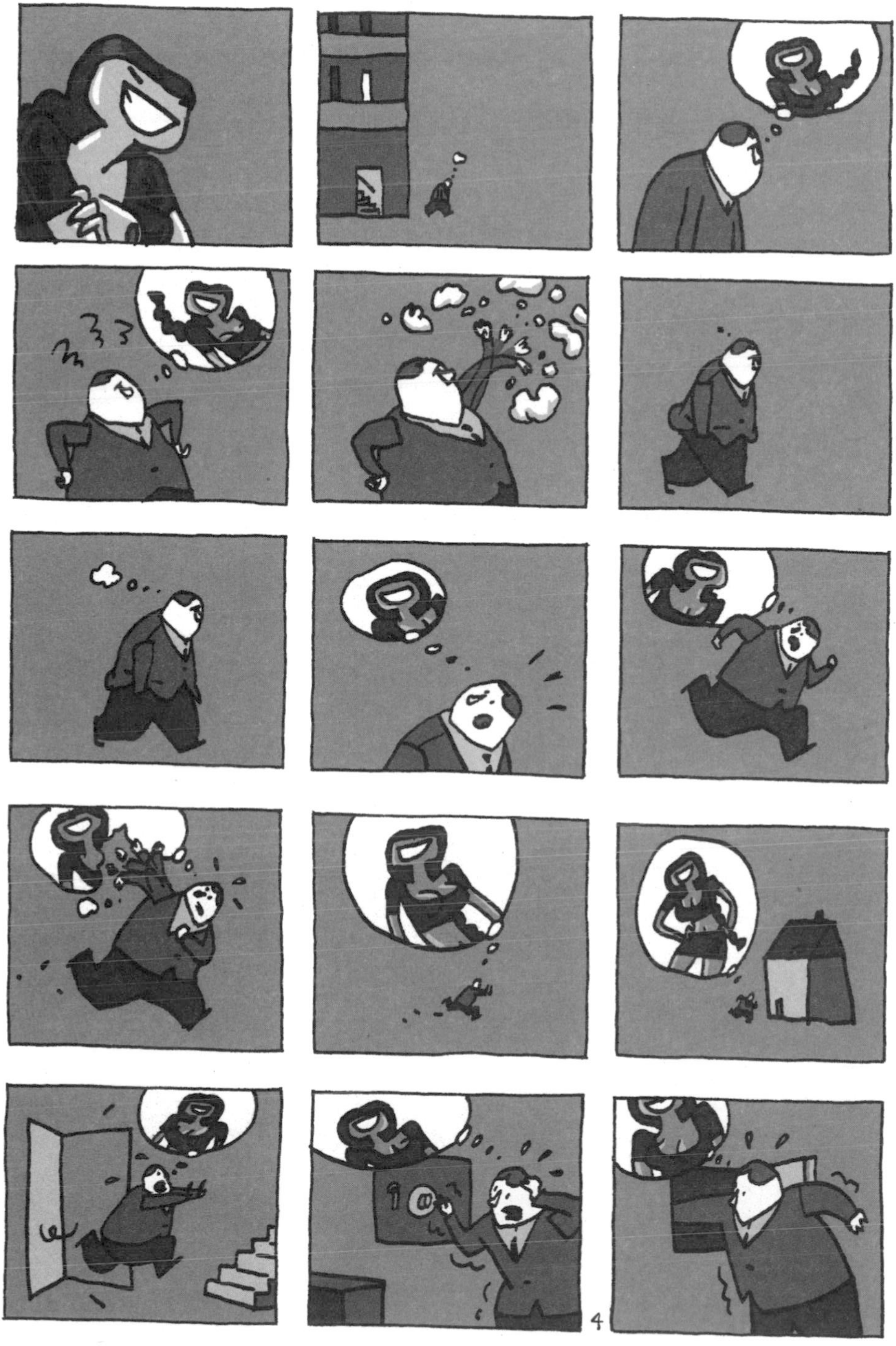

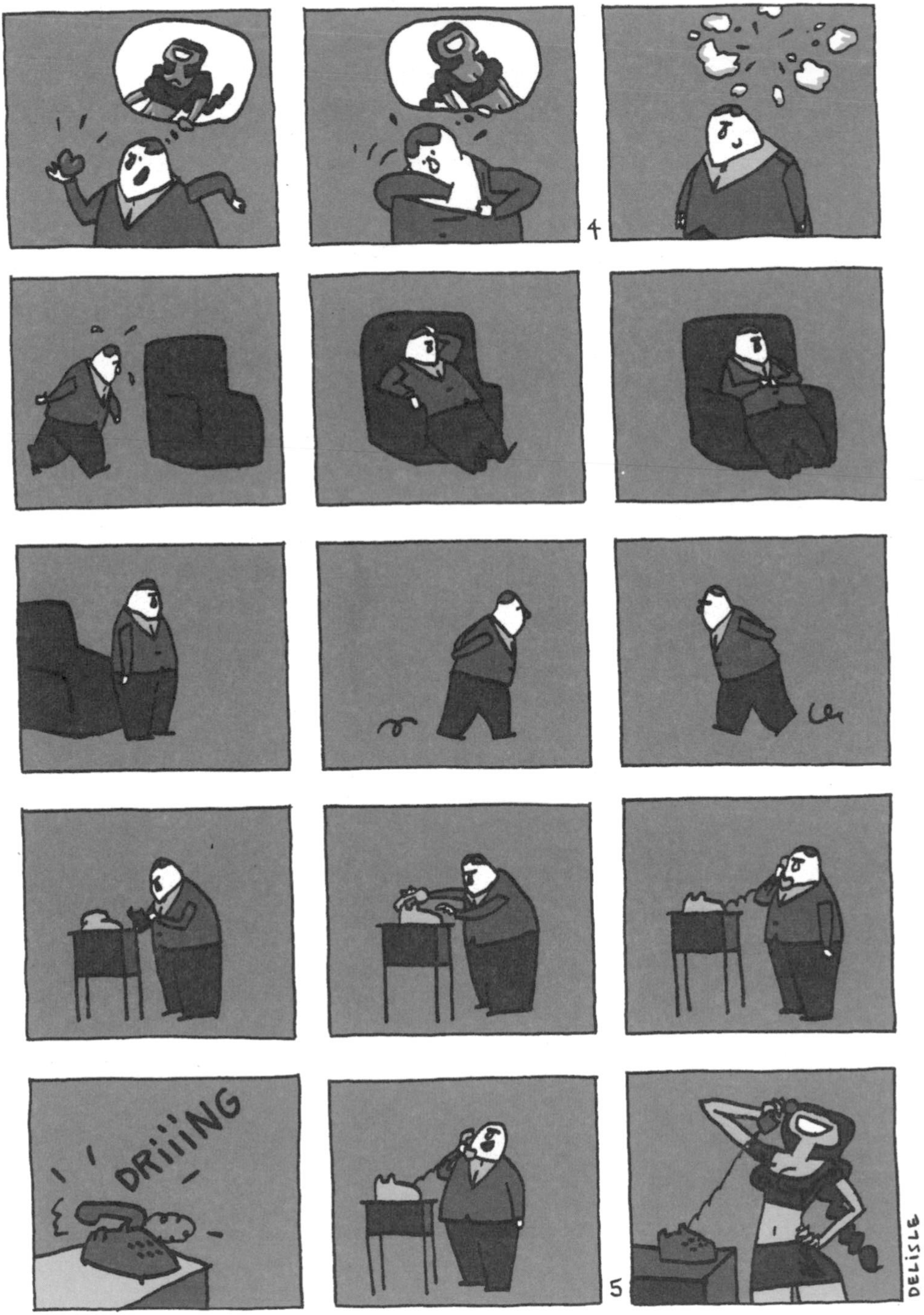
4
DRiiiNG
5
DELISLE

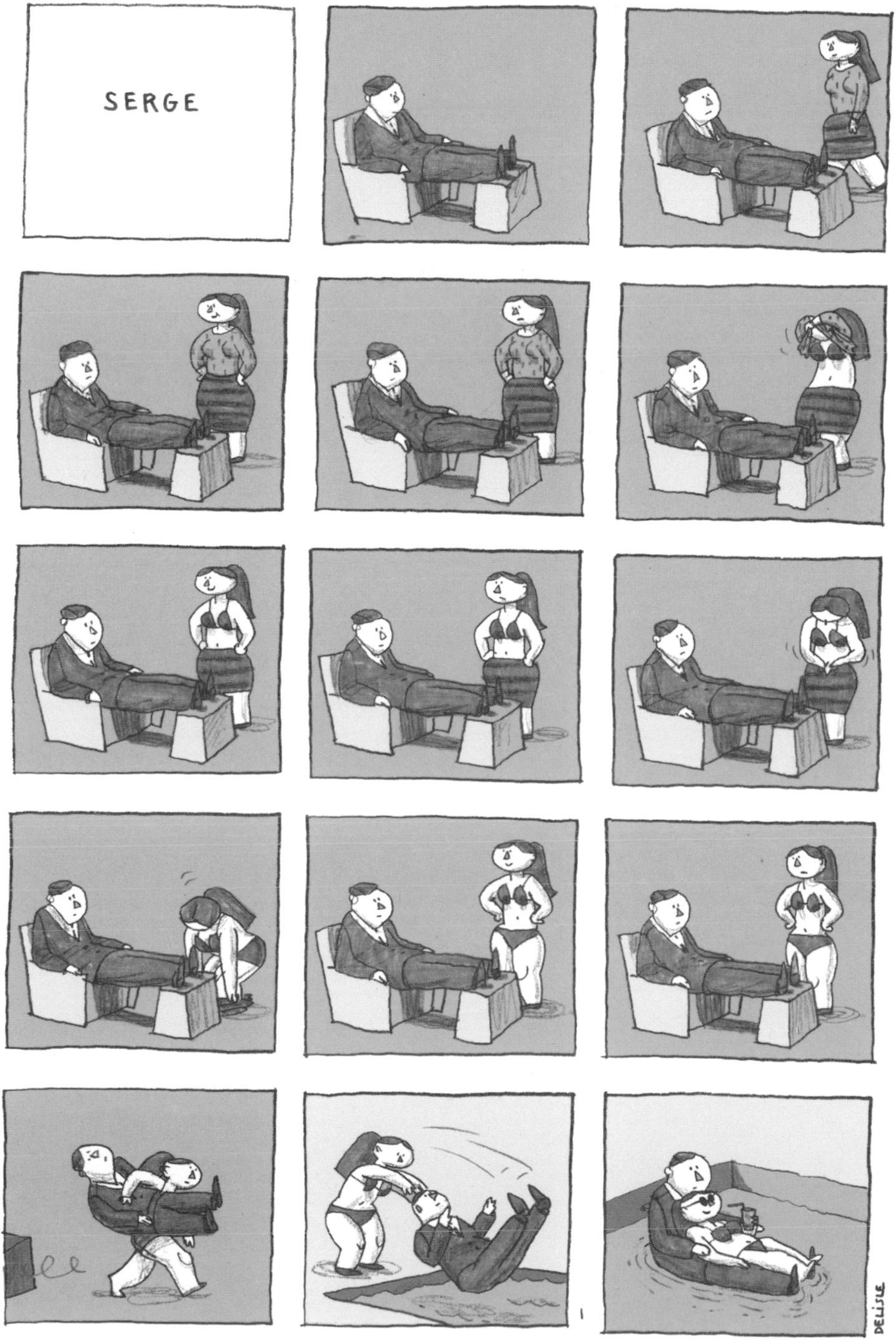
SERGE
DELISLE

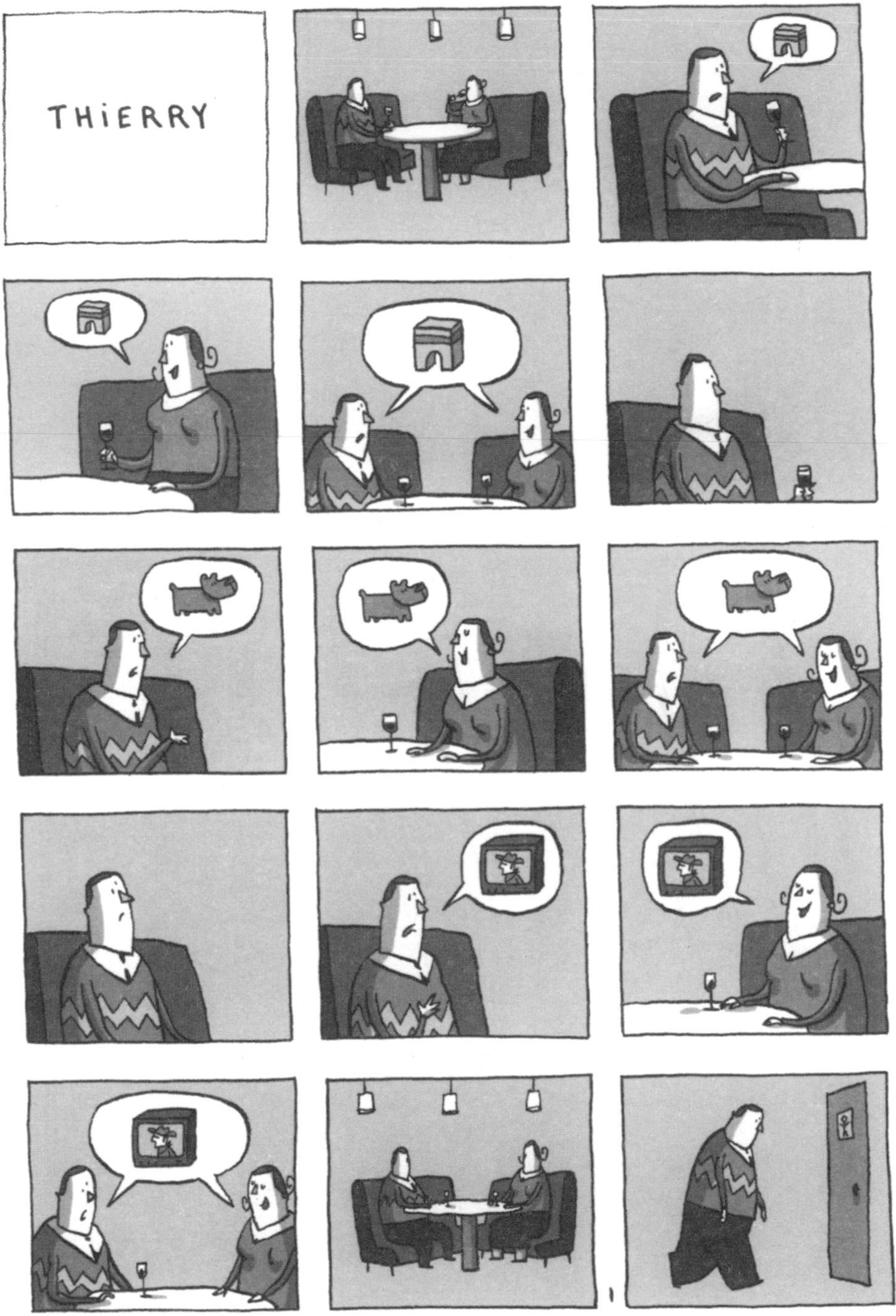
THiERRY

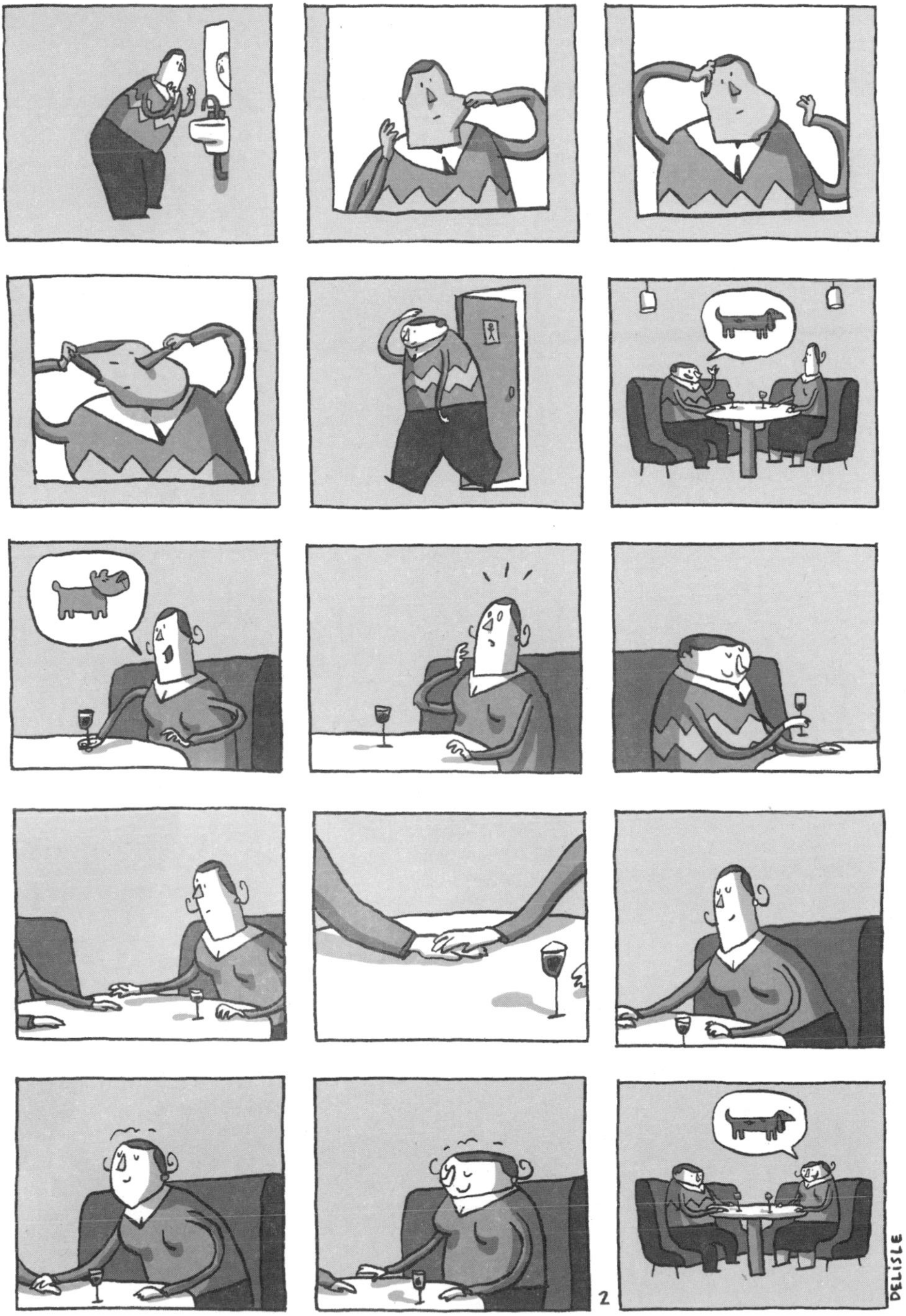
DELISLE

URBAIN

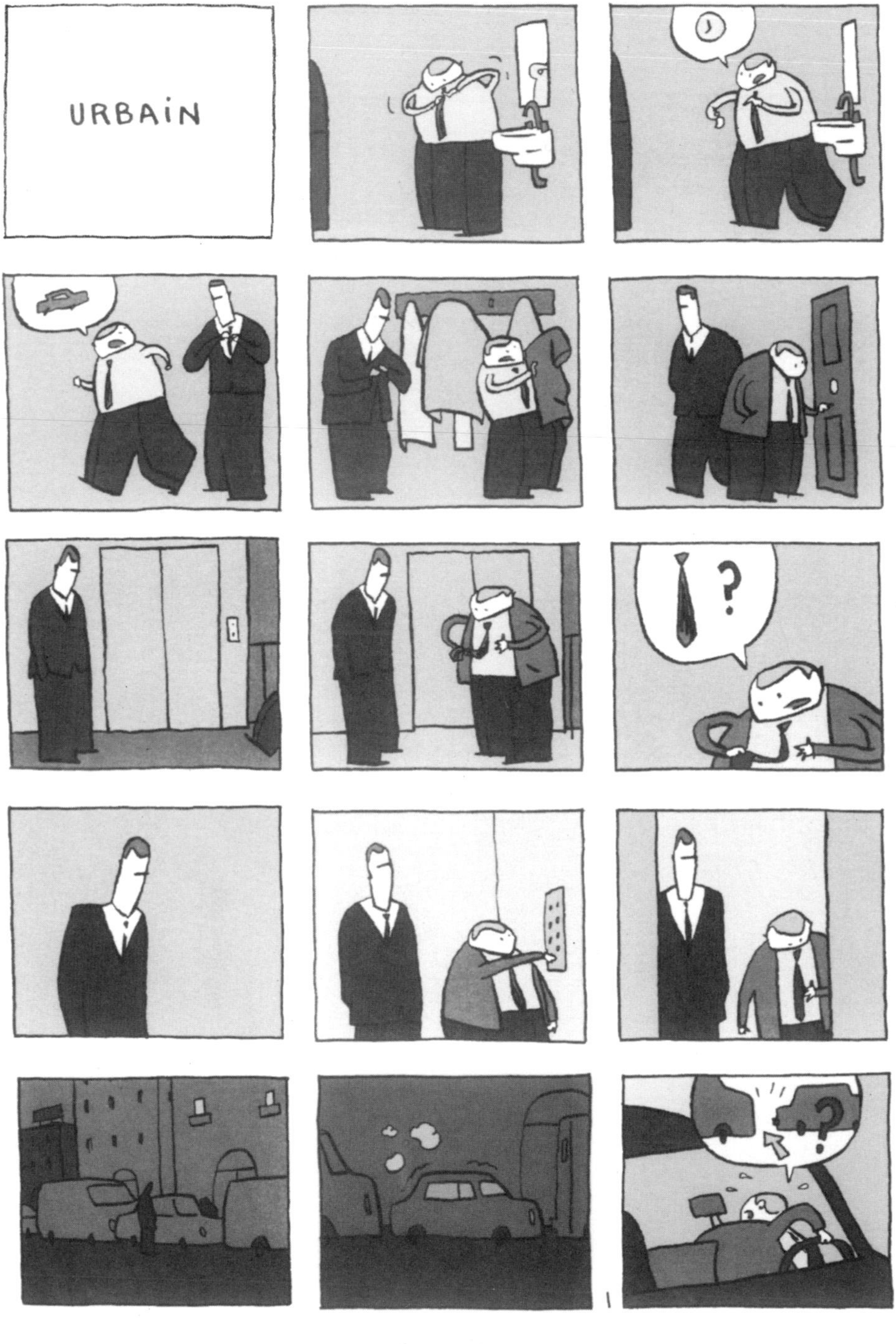
?
?

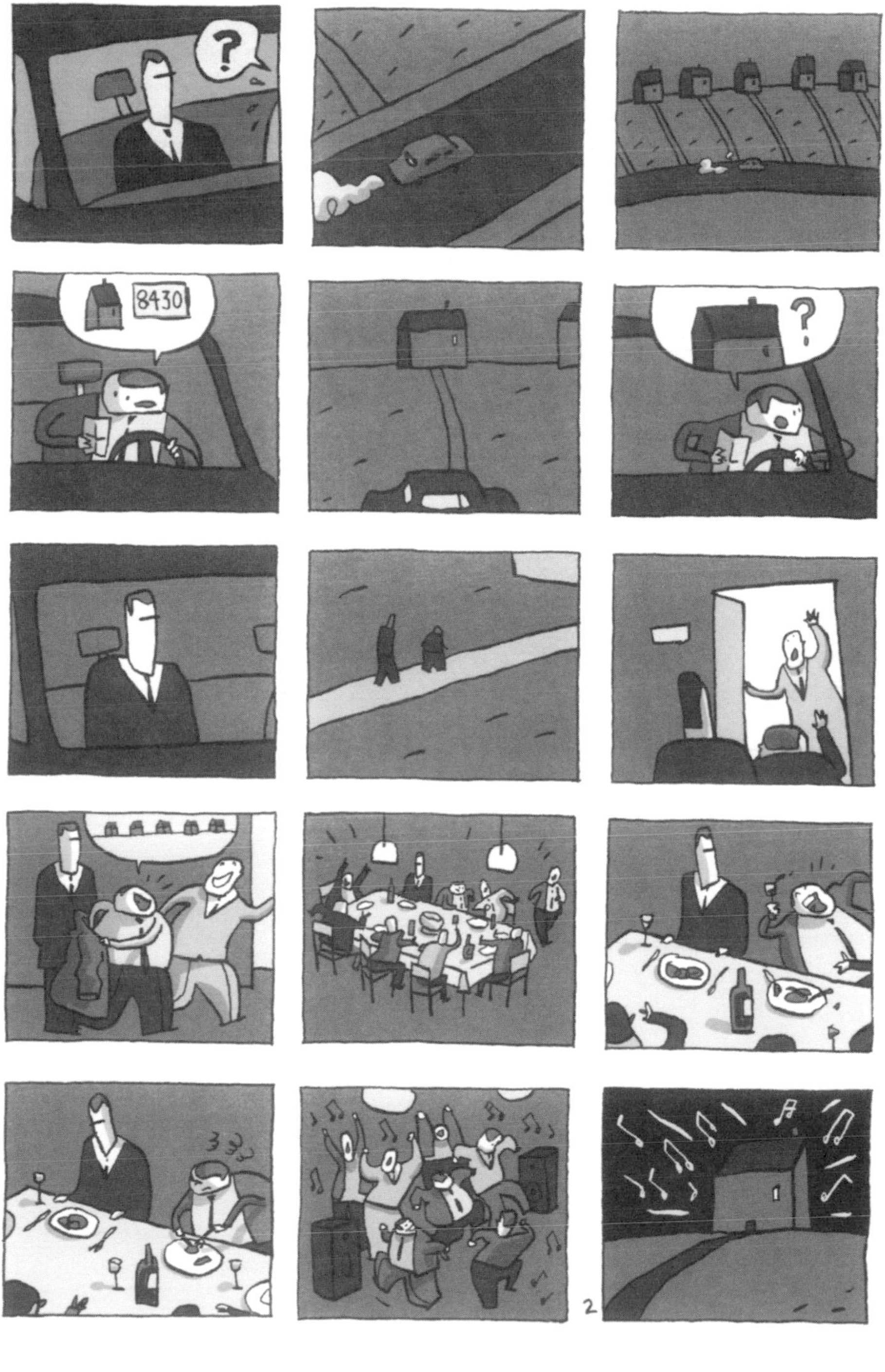
?
8430
?

3

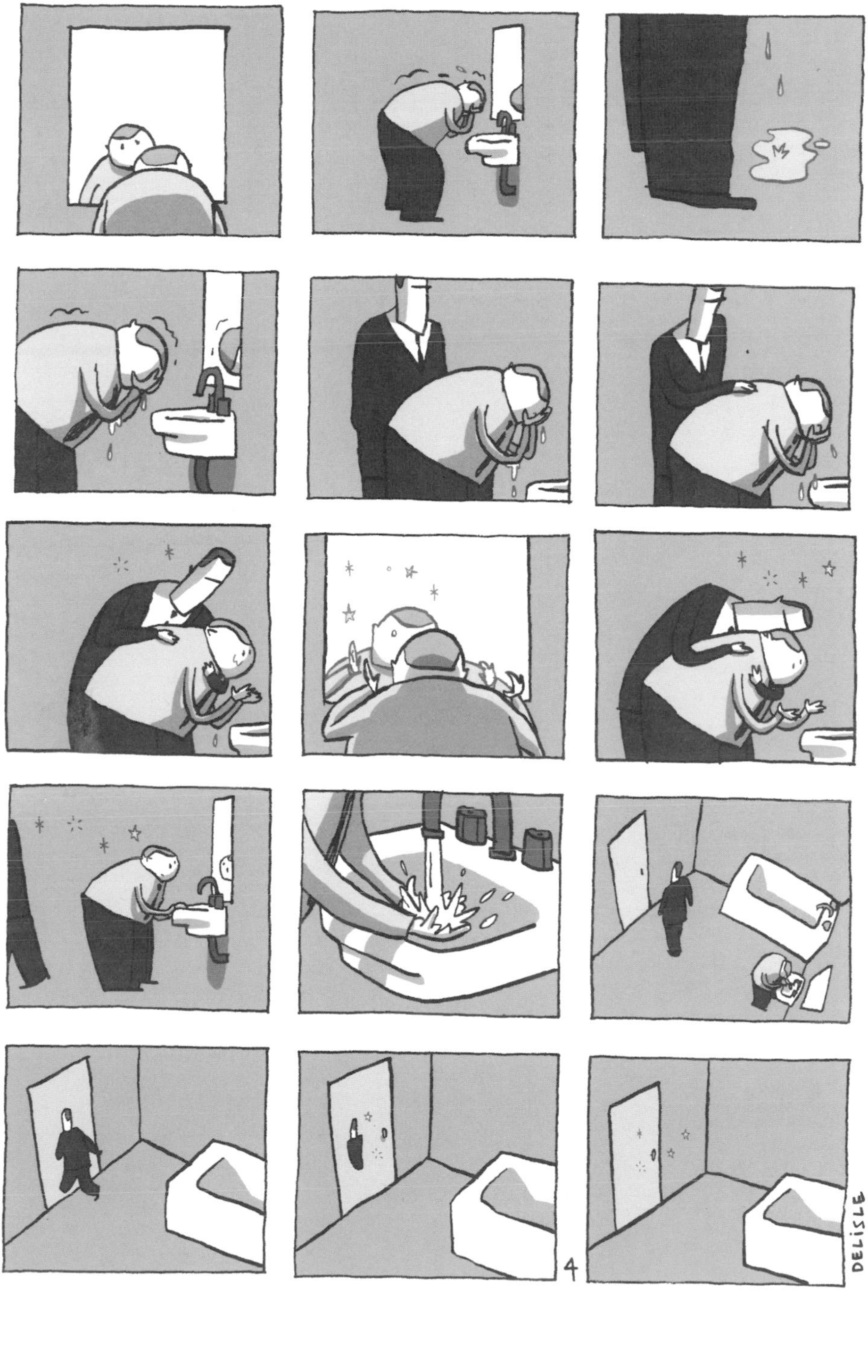
DELISLE

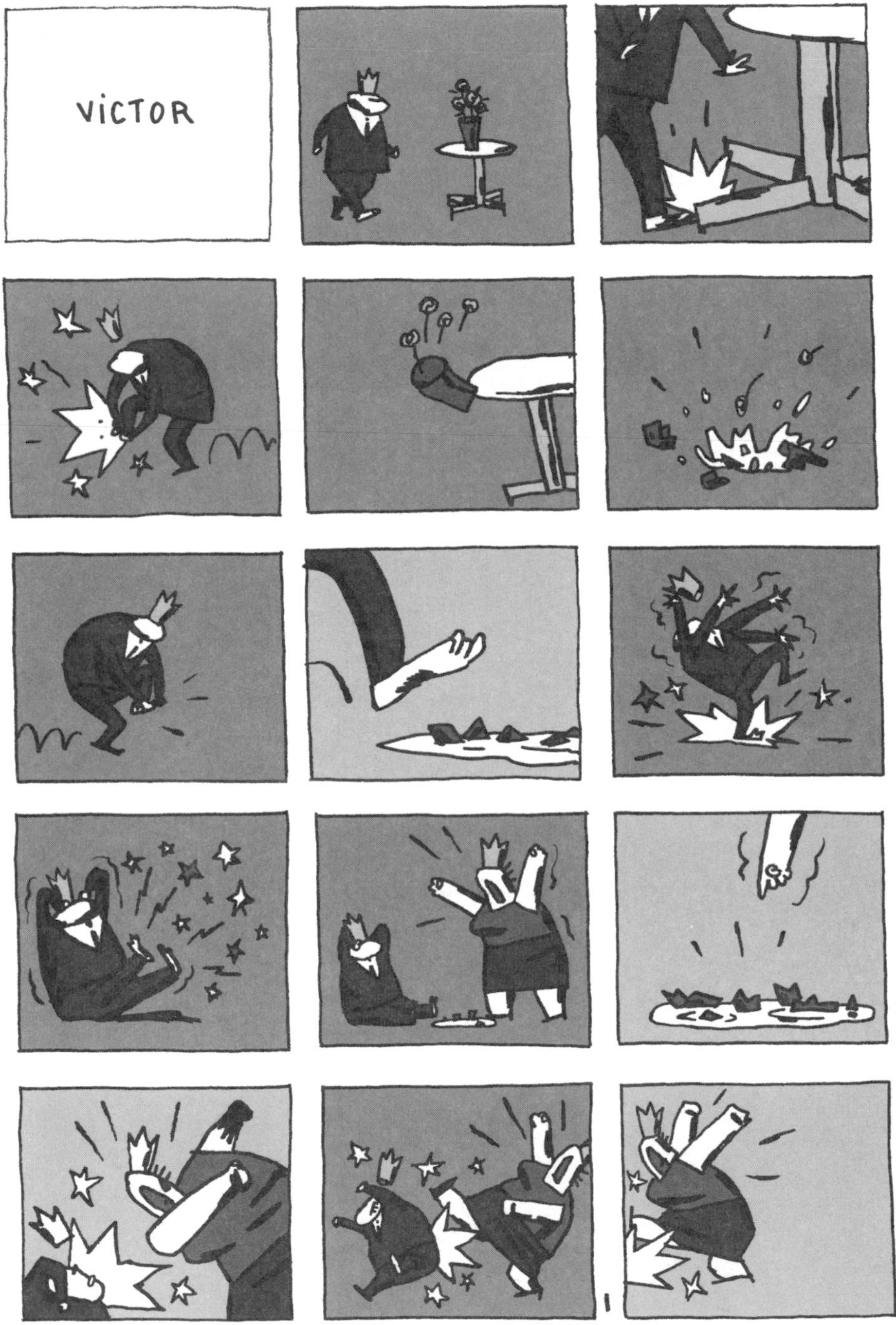
VICTOR

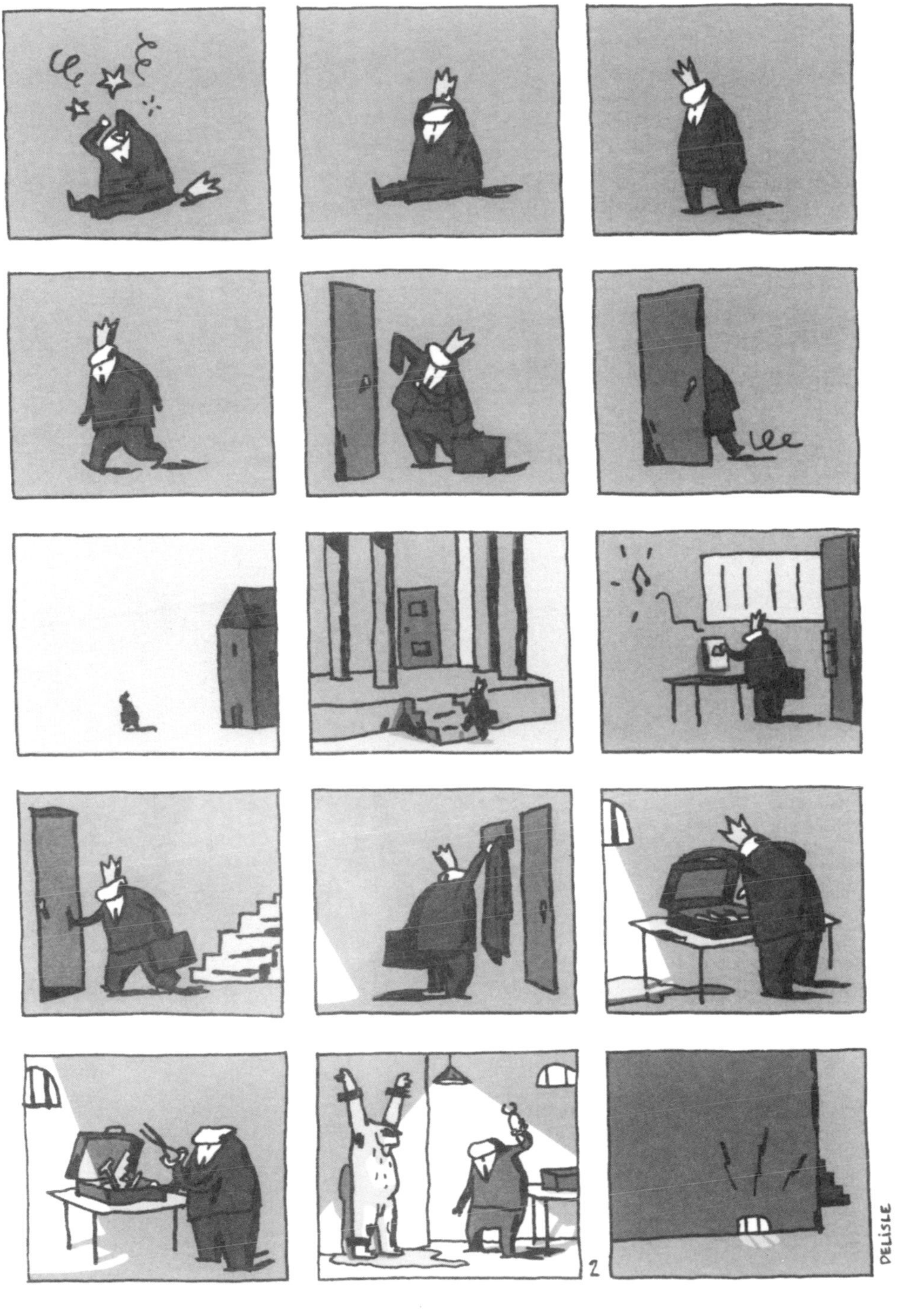
2
DELISLE

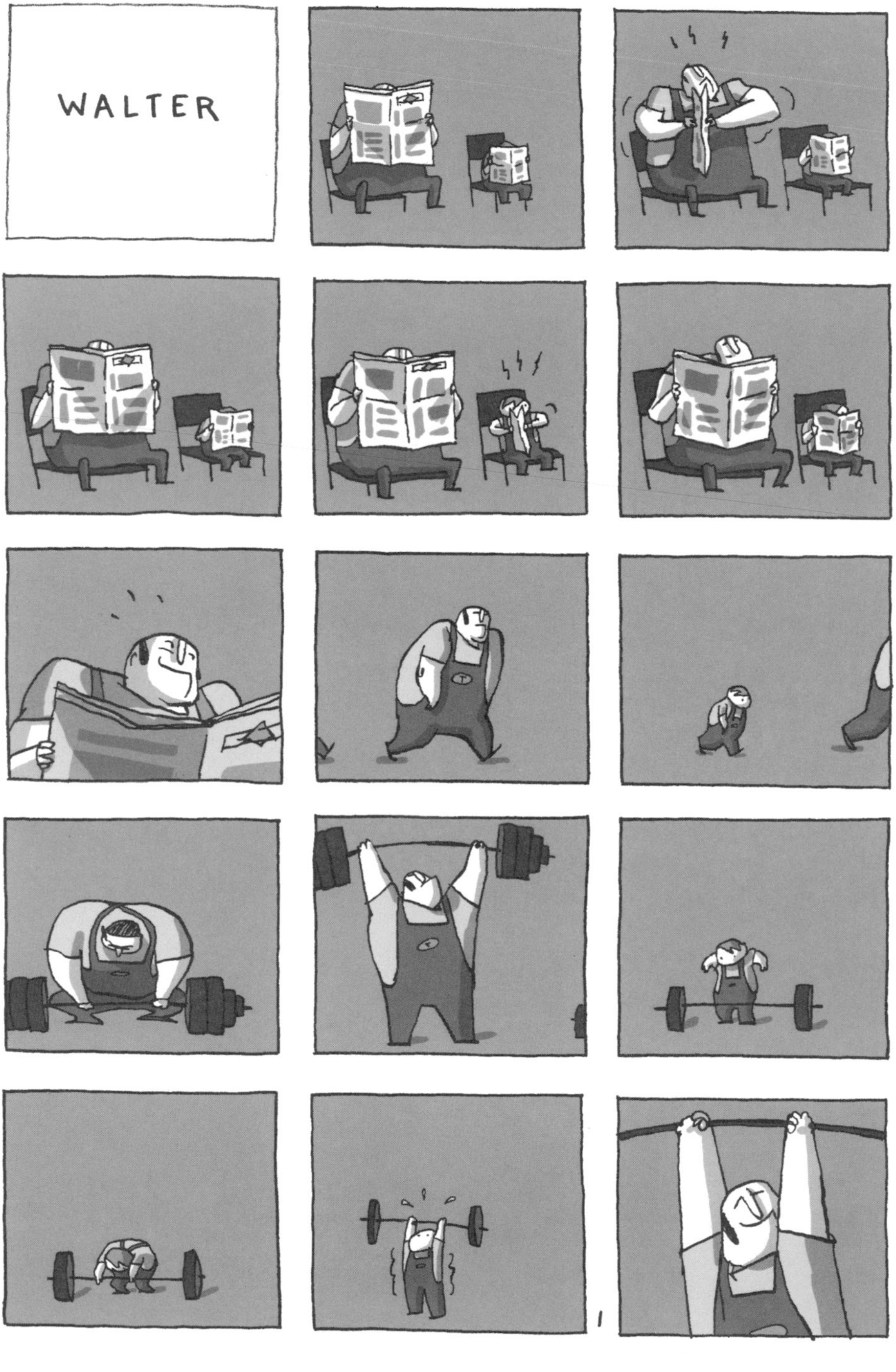
WALTER

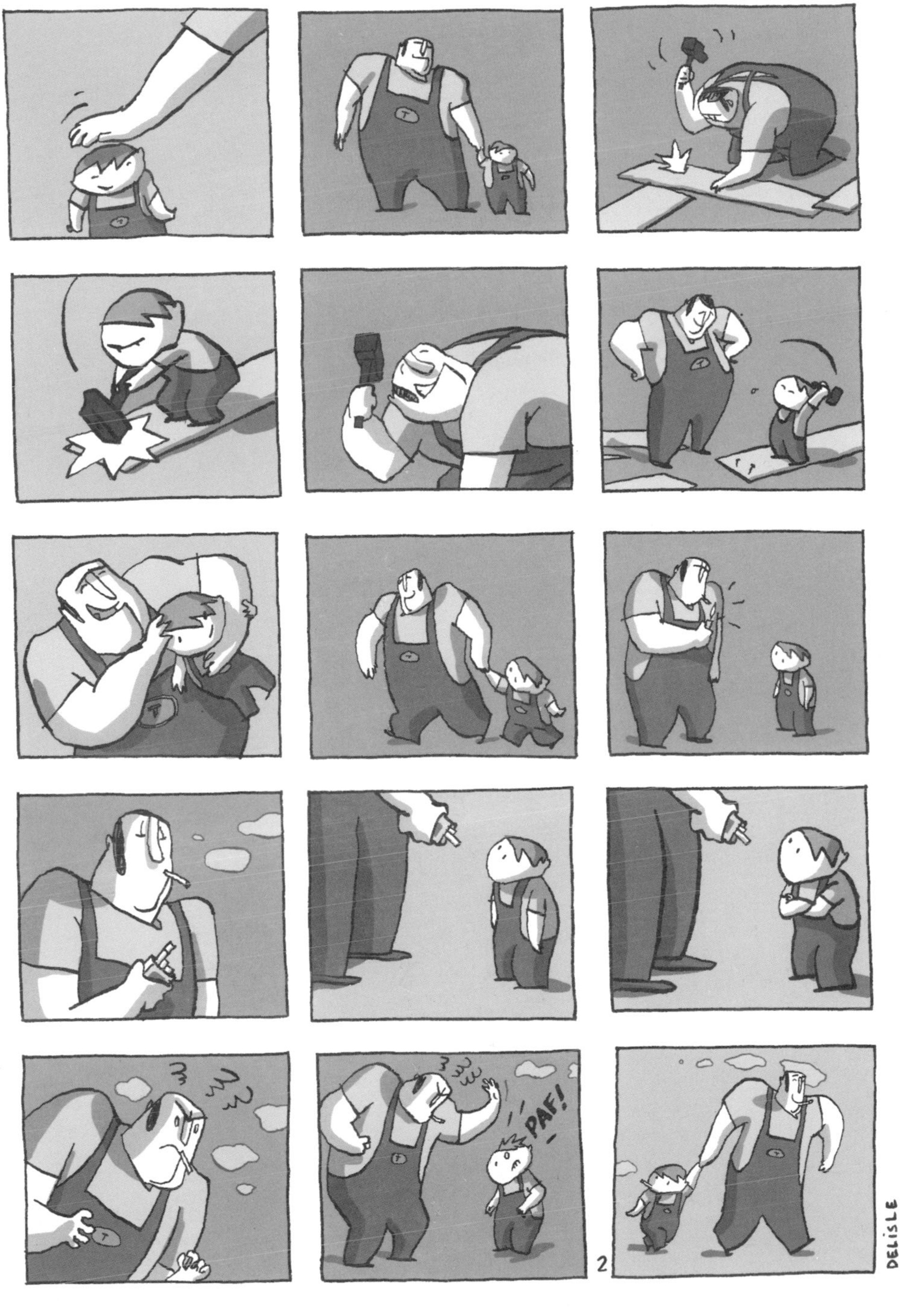
PAF!
DELISLE

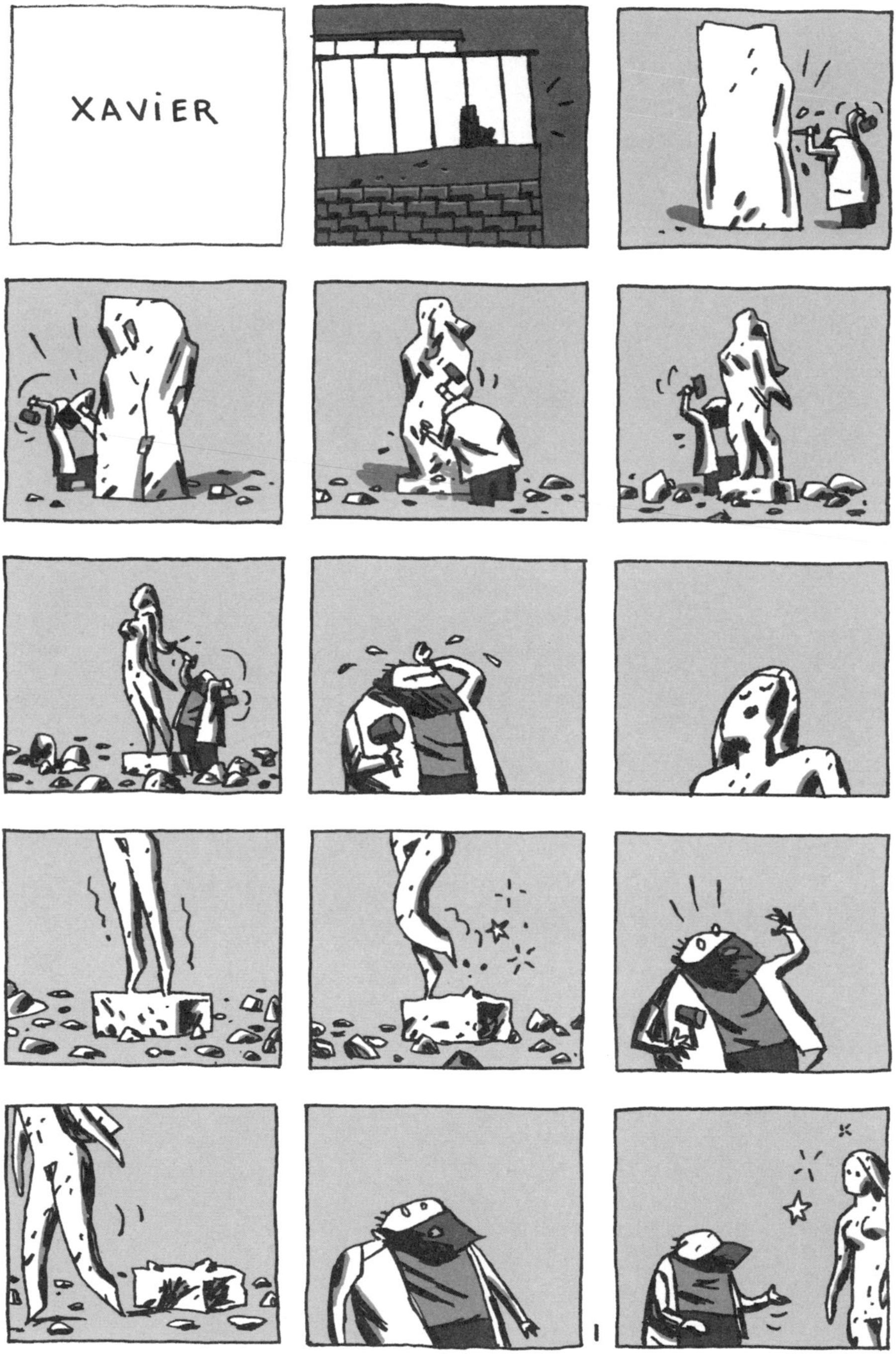
XAVIER

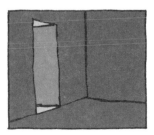

2

DELISLE

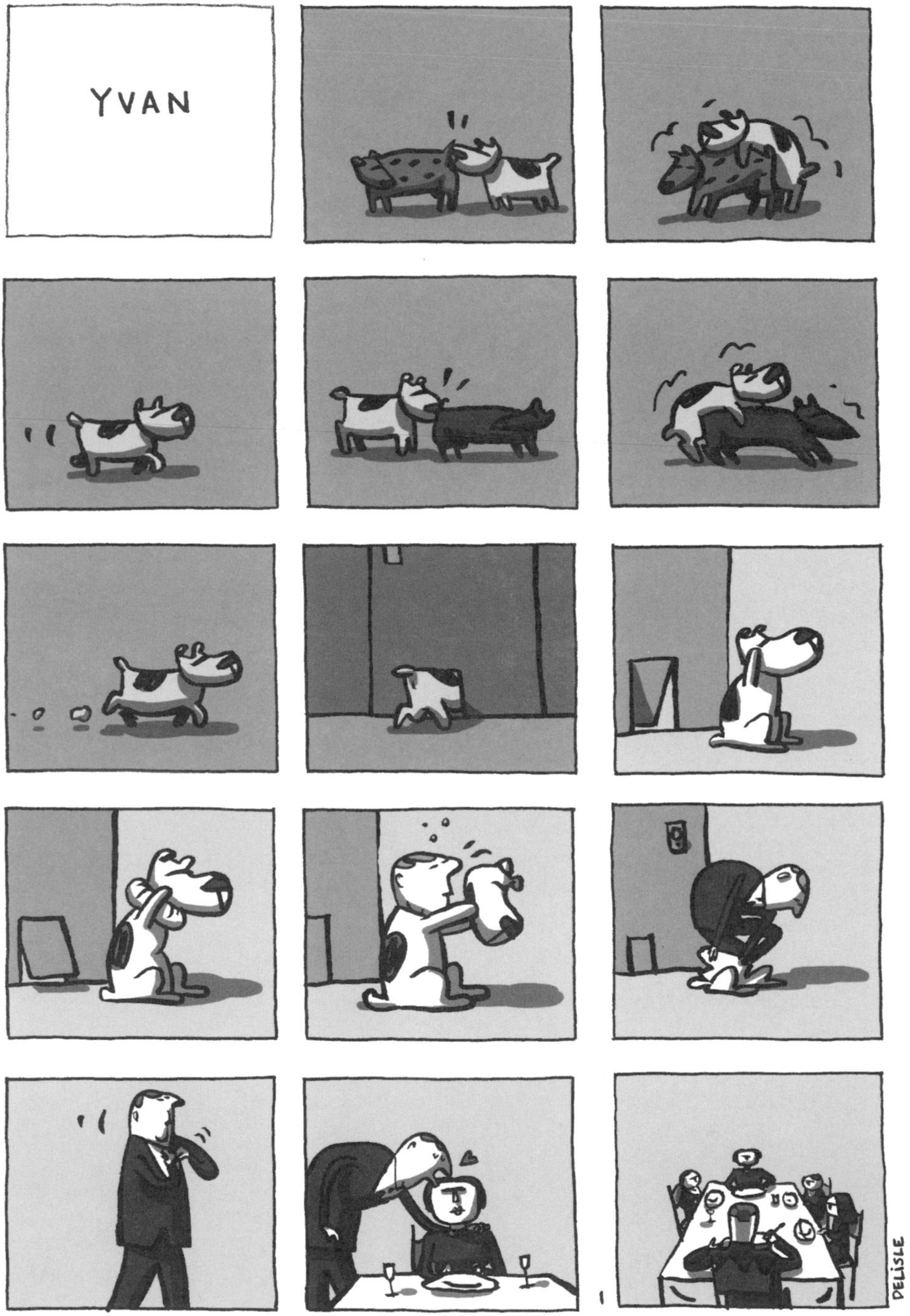
YVAN
DELISLE

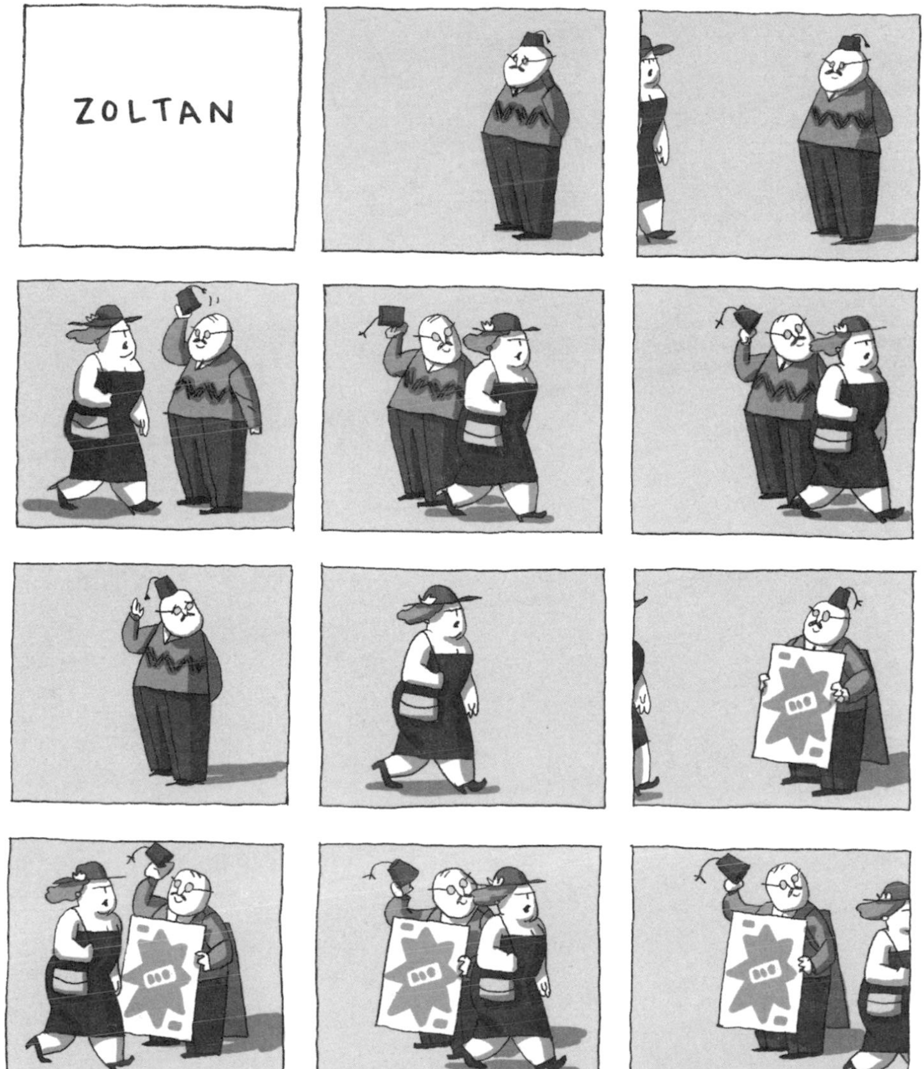
ZOLTAN

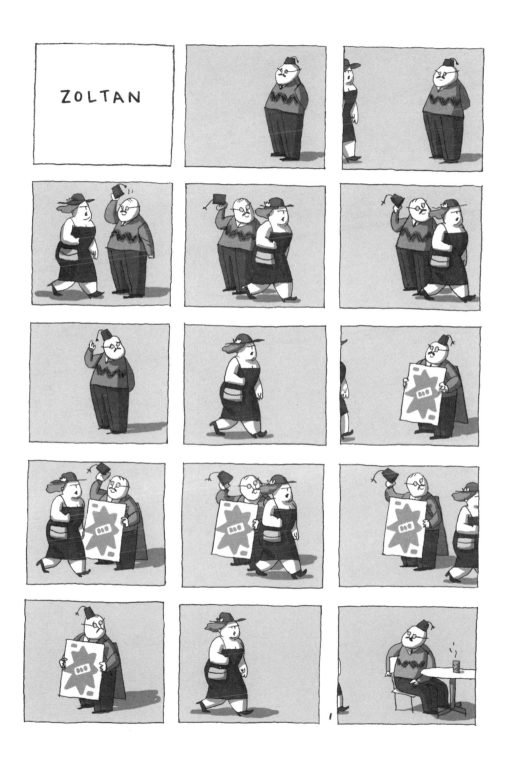

2

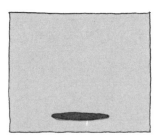

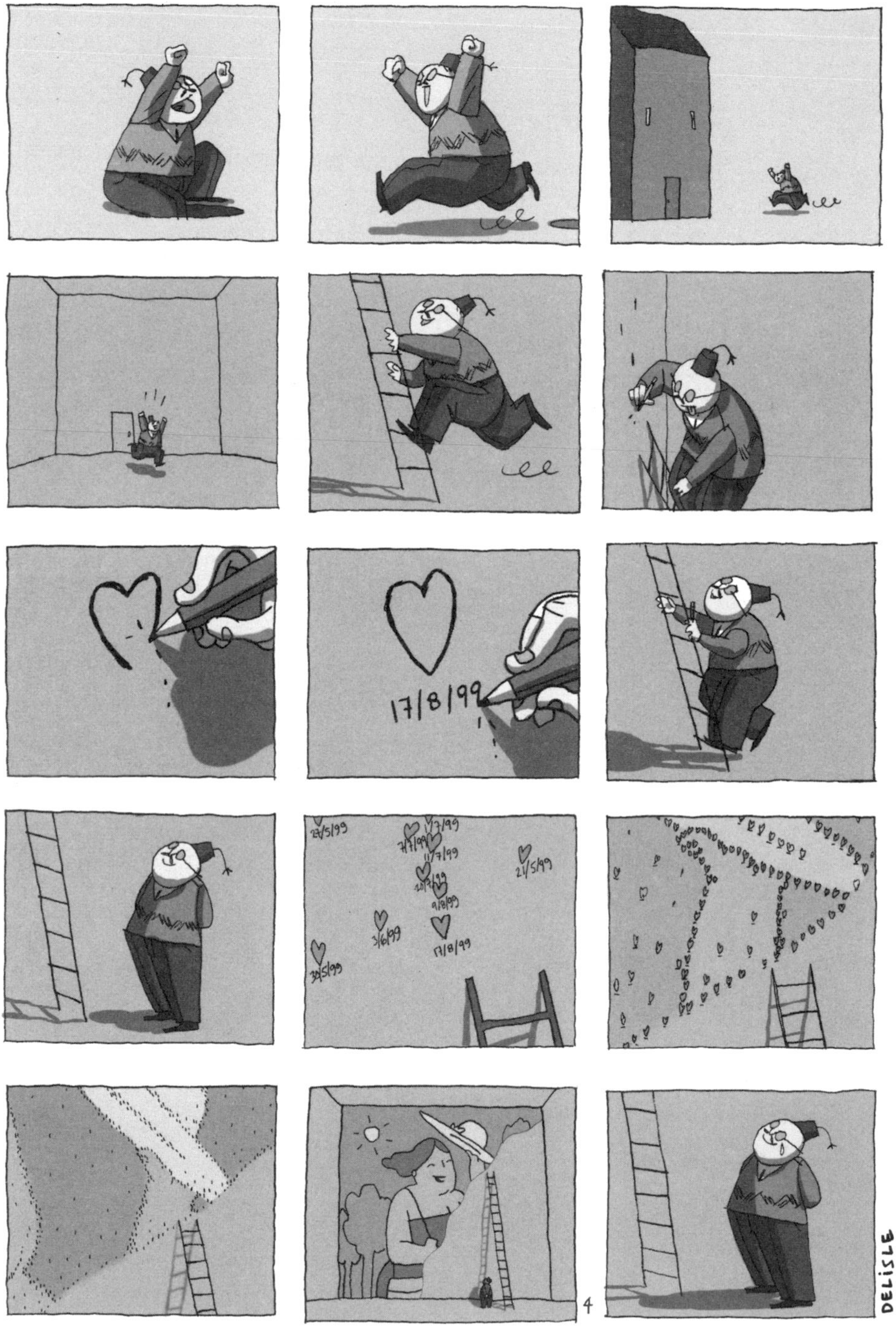
17/8/99
21/5/99
3/6/99
17/8/99
DELISLE

ALBERT 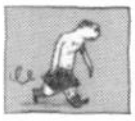

BERNARD 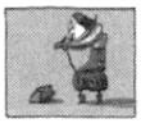

CHRISTOPHE 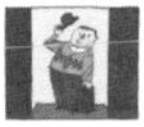

DAVID 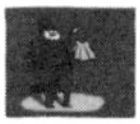

ÉTIENNE 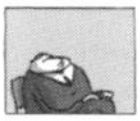

FERNAND 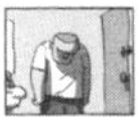

GEORGES 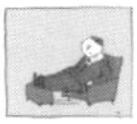

HENRI 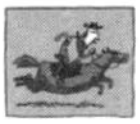

ISIDORE 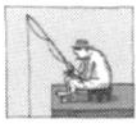

JEAN-LUC 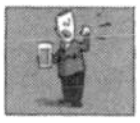

KLEBERT 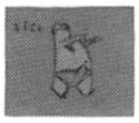

LUCIEN 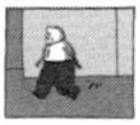

MATHIEU 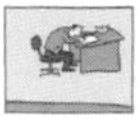

NORBERT 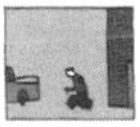

OLIVIER 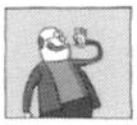

PHILIPPE 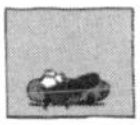

QUENTIN 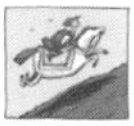

ROBERT 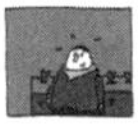

SERGE 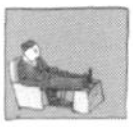

THIERRY 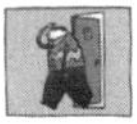

URBAIN 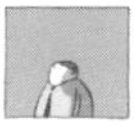

VICTOR 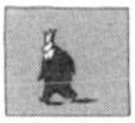

WALTER 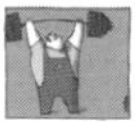

XAVIER 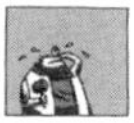

YVAN 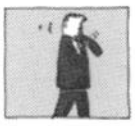

ZOLTAN 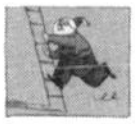